NAHC Member Tips

NAHC Member Tips

North American Hunting Club
Minneapolis, Minnesota

NAHC Member Tips

North American Hunting Club:
Executive Director: Bill Miller
Vice President, Product Marketing: Mike Vail
Product Marketing Director: Cal Franklin
Book Products Development Manager: Steve Perlstein

Design: Todd Brobst, T.H.E. Design Group
Editing: Molly Rose Teuke, Wild Rose Editorial
Cover Photo: Bill Miller

Published by
North American Hunting Club
12301 Whitewater Drive
Minneapolis, MN 55343

ISBN 0-914697-71-4

Printed in U.S.A.

1   2   3   4   5   6   7   9

Contents

Introduction

There are many benefits which make membership in the North American Hunting Club so important to so many hunters around the world! For some members, the key benefit is the "Hunting Reports" program, which offers added assurance when you're setting up a hunt with a guide or outfitter. And we all know, added confidence in your decision can spell the difference in a success or a bust!

Others tout the "Field Test" program as the service from which they derive the most benefit. There isn't another organization out there in which products are put through such rigorous tests by actual club members!

A lot of members like the chance to win hunts and other prizes in the "Great Gear Give-Away" and the annual Membership Drive Contests. Those once-in-a-lifetime trips are definitely worth working for!

Still other members say their favorite part of the Club is North American Hunter magazine and the "Member Shots" pages. In fact, in all the member surveys over the years, North American Hunter always shows up as the #1 benefit of the NAHC.

The great thing about membership in the North American Hunting Club is that for one low price, you get access to all the benefits and services. You can choose to use them as you need them; all of them are ready and waiting when you do! They are just a phone call, letter, fax or e-mail away!

But perhaps the greatest benefit, one that's seldom even mentioned or even thought of, is simply the camaraderie of belonging to a group of more than three-quarter of a million hunters who feel the same way about hunting as you do. Through the Club and on their own NAHC members share the thrills, excitement and passion of hunting with each other every single day of the year. It's contagious!

NAHC members really care about their fellow members. They want to help each other enjoy the wonderful experiences and memories that hunting has provided each one of them over the years.

That sharing of the hunting experience is what the book you have in your hands is all about. It's a compilation of tips, hints and pointers submitted by NAHC members just like you. And it's all done for one important purpose. That is to help fellow North American Hunting Club members enjoy their hunting more.

That's the spirit in which NAHC members submitted their tips and that's the spirit in which the Club decided to publish this book.

Longtime members have heard and read it many times! The most basic goal of the NAHC has always been to enhance the hunting skill, enjoyment, safety and ethics of its members. This book is yet another step down that well-defined trail.

Learn. Enjoy. Hunt safely. We hope this book and your membership in the North American Hunting Club help you do just that.

Best afield,

Bill Miller

Bill Miller
Executive Director

Game

Locating Mule Deer

To discover the location of any mule deer bedded nearby, I blow several loud blasts on a predator call. For some reason, mule deer often stand up to investigate the sound. At that point, I either shoot or plan my stalk.

Amos S. Gingerich
Paoli, Indiana

The Wisconsin Deer Rope

A group of us hunt the woods and river bottoms of Northern Wisconsin. We each carry a rope that is six feet long and three-eighths inch in diameter. It has a wooden handle on one end, and a loop on the other.

When we bag a deer, we loop the rope around the deer's rack and pull using the wooden handle. One or two people can easily pull the deer out this way. Also, in an emergency, everyone's rope can be looped together to make one long rope.

Ferdinand Schneider
Rhinelander, Wisconsin

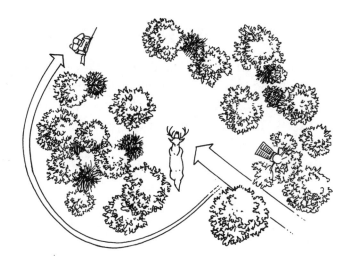

The Solo Approach

One day I was trying to get a shot at a whitetail holed up in a thicket. After an hour of trying to get a clear shot, I decided to try something different.

I left an article of clothing upwind of the thicket, then quietly circled downwind. With the wind in my face, I crawled on hands and knees into the thicket. About halfway through, I saw the deer and made my shot.

Rowland J. Lavallee
Oxbow, Maine

Deer In Turkey Habitat

I deer hunt in an area with a healthy turkey population. To camouflage the noise I make while walking into the woods, I carry a push-button turkey call. When I snap a twig or walk through some noisy brush, I give a few soft clucks. Or if turkeys in the area are yelping, I give a couple of yelps. Deer in the area seem to think I'm one of the flock.

Harold Bennett, Jr.
Wayne, West Virginia

A Bright Idea

I was deer hunting in the Alabama River Swamp at daybreak when I saw two small bucks and a few does. Then there was no action.

I decided to climb a pine ridge and go north to a deer trail. The trail eventually dropped down into a swamp. The timing was perfect! The sun was like a floodlight shining into the swamp.

I was easing along when I saw glints of sunshine off a buck's rack. The buck was feeding and looking straight at me, but he was blinded by the sun. I took a rest on a small tree and squeezed off a shot.

Approximately 95 yards away, I walked up to a fine eight-point whitetail. Anytime I stalk through a swamp or open woodlot and the wind is in my favor, I always put the sun to my back and stalk slowly.

S. E. White-Spunner, Jr.
Mobile, Alabama

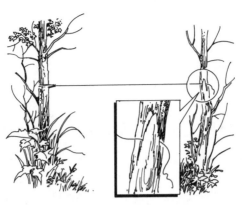

A Better Trail Monitor

When using thread to monitor deer movement on a trail, I tie one end securely to a tree or sapling. On the opposite side of the trail, rather than simply tying the end of the string to a tree, I cut a downward slit in a sapling and pull the thread down tightly in the slit.

When game passes through, the thread pulls out instead of breaking and I can quickly fasten the string back into the slit.

George Smith
Georgetown, Ohio

Anticipating A Deer's Next Move

When stalking a white-tailed deer, especially one that is feeding, I watch its tail rather than its head. An undisturbed deer will invariably twitch its tail before lifting its head. It also will twitch its tail before lowering its head.

Allan Raw
Rothsay, Minnesota

How To Stop A Buck

I was still-hunting through the woods with my muzzle-loader. At noon, I heard a deer running toward me. The buck appeared about 30 yards away, and it looked like he was going to run right past me.

Not having time for any other option, I gave a quick whistle when he was 15 yards away. This curious sound caused the deer to stop, which gave me an easy shot.

Tim Slover
Rogersville, Missouri

A Mirror Can Push A Buck

Many survival manuals stress the use of a mirror to attract attention or to signal for assistance. One added bonus is often overlooked.

I have found the shine from a mirror, properly placed, can cause a buck to stand up or to move. This works especially well on mule deer.

Some hunters throw rocks into draws and canyons. The mirror has the added advantage that I can be selective as to which animal I "shine." I use a mirror from an old make-up kit.

Gordon J. Poppitt
Westminster, California

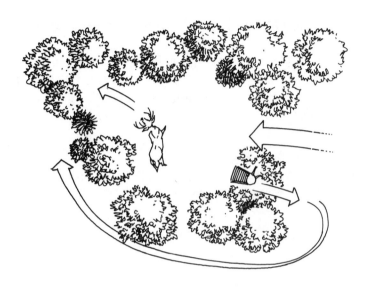

A Tracking Trick

When a deer track suddenly turns downwind, the deer may be going to bed down, probably on the nearest piece of high ground.

I don't follow a track that turns downwind. Instead, I back up about 100 yards, then circle downwind of the track. I stalk the nearest piece of high ground that overlooks the deer's trail. That is where I most often jump the deer.

Miles Hafner
North Waterford, Maine

Rainy Day Deer Hunt

I don't let a little rain stop me from hunting. I use a "mini" or "handbag" umbrella. It measures 14 inches closed and 32 inches open and sells for under $5. An umbrella like this is great in a tree stand or ground blind. I stash one in a plastic bag at my favorite hunting spots.

I like the maroon color best. Deer don't seem to be alarmed by this color. I have seen deer while walking on logging roads or crossing open fields with the umbrella open.

Paul P. De Lorenzo
Rome, New York

Avoid Buck Fever

One method I use to help prevent buck fever is to imagine a target on the deer. Before going hunting, I look at a lot of deer pictures and pinpoint the best area to shoot. If I'm reading one of my hunting magazines, I draw a target on the deer. I teach myself to automatically think about the target. For me, this works.

John C. Roberts
Dadeville, Alabama

Fence-line Whitetails

One of my favorite places to set up my tree stand is along a fence line between fields. These fence lines often contain well-used trails. Deer use these paths because sometimes they are totally hidden from roads and hillsides.

The secret to bringing deer down a trail like this is a good cover scent. I pour the scent into a spray bottle and wear knee-high rubber boots. I spray the soles of my boots, then start down the trail. About every ten feet I spray the ground or brush. If there is a good crosswind, I sometimes spray the air.

I follow this pattern to my stand, where I scrape up the dirt with a stick. I spray that spot several times, and then climb into my stand. I place my stand high enough so that I can see most of the path between the fields. What a thrill to see bucks and does following that path, sniffing the ground cautiously as they walk down the trail. This method works well for me.

David Burch
Lynchburg, Virginia

To Hunt Bucks, Find Does

We try to concentrate as many does in one area as possible. We use feeders on the Texas ranch we hunt.

I hunt at the base of a mountain, and use two feeders set up 250 yards away from my tower blind. The feeders are about 250 yards apart and are in tight cover so the deer won't feel pressured.

When the rut is in full swing, the hunter who has the most does in his area will likely have the most buck traffic.

Wyndle Wright
Frisco, Texas

Deer Crossing Tips

Here are some tips I've learned when hunting deer at a crossing, whether it is a fence, logging road, waterway or whatever.

- I set up 30 to 50 yards away from the crossing. If deer are shot at or near the crossing, they begin to associate the crossing with danger. The deer will then approach the crossing on full alert or start crossing at another location. Deer that have already made the jump and browsed for 30 to 50 yards have forgotten the crossing and therefore do not associate danger with the crossing.

- Deer will have several points of jumping at a crossing. I set up ground blinds to cover the trail of each jump, and still observe the activity at the other jumps. I have noted that when deer start using one crossing in the morning, other deer will use the same spot. If I am at the wrong place in the morning, I move into a more productive location.

- I construct ground blinds from the limbs I cut to clear shooting lanes, using wire or twine to keep them in place. I build a full backdrop that I cannot see through. This allows for a quartering-away shot after the deer has passed me. I do not see the deer until it is in a shooting position, which gives me less time to get nervous and less time for the deer to spot me. I also leave cover in front of my position to help break up my outline.

    – I never allow the wind to blow my scent to the approaching deer. If I can't be downwind, I don't hunt the blind. The most I can hope for is to confuse the animal with cover scents. I use whatever strong natural odors are in the area like juniper, loco weed or broom weed. These scents leave a strong, pungent odor when rubbed into clothing. On boots I apply a cover scent of a small animal that is prominent in the area, such as quail, rabbit or raccoon. I purchase these scents from dog training supply stores or sporting good stores. I also use sheep or other livestock droppings to cover my movement in an area.

    – When entering my crossing area, I plan several approach and departure routes. If I fail to alter my approach, the deer will pattern me just like I pattern them.

Jonnie L. York
Arlington, Texas

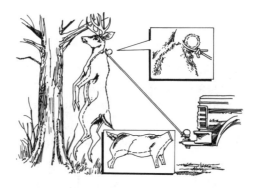

Skinning Deer

The meat processor our family uses takes only skinned deer. We have been asked several times how we skin our deer without getting cut marks or hair on the meat. The processor wishes everyone skinned deer this way.

Our old hunting buddy, Phil Breslin, showed us this technique. Do not use this technique on a deer head that will be mounted.

1. Cut around each leg at the knee joint.

2. Cut the hide from the knee joint up to the cut made when field dressing the animal.

3. Continue the cut made when field dressing the animal up to the base of the head.

4. Cut around the base of the head.

5. Skin the hide away from the neck, then place a rock under the hide at the back of the neck.

6. Hang the deer by its head and tie a sturdy rope around the rock and hide.

7. Tie the rope to a truck or ATV, and slowly pull away. The hide will peel off very easily.

Jerry Grill
Fowlerville, Michigan

Cattle Impact Deer

Years of hunting farmland has taught me that deer don't like to be around cattle. Perhaps the cattle are too noisy, too active or too smelly.

Deer seem to become edgy when cattle move into an area. Therefore, I keep cattle activity in mind when deer hunting, and try to use it to my advantage. That farmer's Holstein may push a bedded buck out of a field or woodlot.

David Bartch
Stockton, Illinois

A Quiet Blind

Just before the rifle season opens, I scout the woods. I select places for ground blinds and clear the ground of leaves, sticks and brush. I place a large plastic bag over the cleared area and anchor it down with rocks or twigs poked through it into the ground. I then place orange surveyor's tape on a nearby tree to mark the location.

On opening day, I go to my favorite blind, pick up the plastic and have a dry, quiet place to stand or sit. If I shift positions or move my foot slightly, I will not make any noise that might alert deer to my presence.

Claude Quick, Jr.
Belvidere, Vermont

Swamp Hunt In Comfort

I deer hunt in the swamps of eastern North Carolina, and I grew tired of coming home with wet socks, boots and pants.

Now I wear waders when I hunt. They are quiet, waterproof and warm. They are available in almost all sporting goods stores, and range in price from $20 to $130. Waders also come in various camouflage patterns.

Thomas Tayloe
Raleigh, North Carolina

A Simple, Multipurpose Wind Indicator

Sometimes, hunters must go deep into the woods to get a trophy buck. Big deer almost always like the thick stuff. In thick cover, determining wind direction can be difficult. Small pieces of string are good at showing wind direction, but they are easily pulled off by the occasional briar patch.

I've found a better wind indicator is a small butane lighter. Its flame will detect the slightest breeze. Besides that, on cold days I have a portable fire in my pocket.

Earl Hertlein, III
Wabash, Indiana

14

A Quiet Meal

Have you ever had a deer spook while trying to open a bag of chips or unwrap a candy bar? I have.

To remedy this, I remove all noisy food wrappers before venturing out for a day's hunt. I put the food into thin plastic bags, or I simply wrap it up in a cloth bandanna.

Thomas S. Brink
Plymouth, Wisconsin

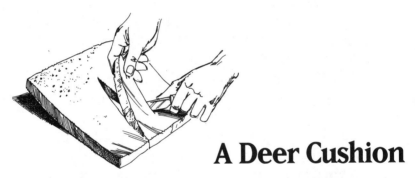

A Deer Cushion

I love hunting whitetails on the ground with my bow. I slip along until I find a likely spot, then I sit down. I travel light, but I like to sit without my south end getting cold or wet.

I find seat cushions tend to be bulky and noisy. Instead, I take a thin seat cushion, cut a V-notch out of the bottom and then slide it down inside my pants. There is no noise, no fuss, and I am always warm and dry!

Charles A. Laversa
Newburyport, Massachusetts

A Few Tips After 35 Years

I have learned many valuable lessons after 35 years of deer hunting. I have taken 88 deer with a gun and 85 deer with a bow. Here is what I've learned.

- I do not smoke.
- I wear clean clothes every time.
- I wear knee-high rubber boots.
- If there is a poor blood trail and darkness is coming, I try to see the natural travel lanes in the woods. I turn my flashlight off, squint my eyes, or turn my head sideways. After some practice, I will see tunnels. This is what the deer sees. I follow these tunnels and this is where I will find the deer.
- I never sit in the same tree more than three times a year.
- I am quiet whenever I approach and depart my hunting area.
- If I am bowhunting, I practice with broadheads. Broadheads fly differently than field tips.
- When I first started using a grunt tube it was magic. No one else had one. Today, most hunters have a grunt tube, and I get little or no response from deer. Now I use a grunt call to stop a deer for the shot.
- I save money by butchering my own deer. There are very good books and videos that make butchering easy and enjoyable.

Tom O'Connor
Granite Falls, Minnesota

A Noisy Trail Monitor

When I hunt over a game trail, I place two sticks across the trail. I place one about 100 feet up the trail from my stand, and the other about 100 feet down the trail from my stand. I place both sticks about two feet off the ground, between two trees or rocks. The sticks are no thicker than my little finger.

Game often will alert me to their approach by breaking the stick.

Allen Hockaday
Powell, Wyoming

Easy Range Estimation

I carry a roll of fluorescent surveyor's tape when I put up my deer stand. I step off distances from 15 to 30 yards, and mark those distances with small pieces of tape.

When deer come near my stand, I have an easy reference to estimate the distance.

George Smith
Georgetown, Ohio

Leave A Note

I deer hunt with a partner whose stand is several hundred yards away. In addition to the normal hunting equipment, we each carry a waterproof felt pen and a small pad of bright colored note paper. If one of us leaves our stand, we jot a note listing the time and direction of travel. We post it on a nearby branch or tree.

Even when hunting alone, this is good practice. Wise hunters always let someone know where they expect to be. Leaving a note could save precious time in the event of an emergency. Regardless of how inconvenient it might seem, always retrieve the notes.

Christopher W. Cooper
Indianapolis, Indiana

A Homemade Scrape Dripper

I take an empty Elmer's Glue bottle, clean it out and duct tape a piece of stove pipe wire to the bottle. Then I camouflage the bottle with paint, fill it up with my favorite scent and wire it to a branch. I control how fast it drips by adjusting the tip of the bottle.

Steve Furmanski
Crystal Falls, Michigan

A Mobile Scent Dispenser

When baiting black bear, I spread bacon grease on the ground surrounding the bait. When a bear steps in the grease, it gets on the bear's paws.

When the animal walks away from the bait, the bruin will leave a scent trail. This scent trail can be picked up by other bears, which will lead them to the bait.

Thomas S. Brink
Plymouth, Wisconsin

Natural Wind Indicators

Milkweed pods can make great wind indicators. I pick several pods in August and September when they are dry.

During the hunting season, I open the pod, pull out a seed with its fluff attached and let it go. I can watch the air current as it drops, turns, etc. I even spray the pods with my favorite scent.

Paul Blowers
Belington, West Virginia

19

Hunt During A Strong Wind

The best time for me to harvest a trophy mule deer, bull elk or whitetail is during a strong wind. I still-hunt into or across the wind, and try to hunt all day. The wind masks any noise I make. This also allows me to get much closer to the animal. I have taken four quality mule deer during the middle of the day using this technique.

Carl Kiel
Phoenix, Arizona

Map Out Game Data

When buying maps of my favorite big game hunting spots, I always purchase an extra copy.

I use one copy as an ordinary field map. With the second copy, I create a "game data" map. I record information about animals, sign and habitat. Patterns on the game data map soon develop.

Steve Kosek
Bellaire, Ohio

Prune During Winter Months

When scouting during winter months, I take pruning tools along. It is far easier to prune shooting lanes during winter. Also, animals that notice the change will have several months to grow comfortable with the new scenery before hunting season begins.

Shane McNamara
Pictou, Nova Scotia

Set Up By A Stream

When possible, I place my stand next to a small stream. The sound of running water will help cover small noises I make. It may even cover the noise of my shot.

I also use streams as a pathway to my stand. By walking slowly in the water, I can approach my stand quietly. Also, the running water will help carry away my scent. This approach has worked for me many times.

Shane McNamara
Pictou, Nova Scotia

Great-tasting Pronghorn

I was raised on a ranch south of Upton, Wyoming, during the 1930s. My father was an old cowboy. In the summers of 1912 to 1920, he rode with the roundup crews in Montana. Sometimes he lived off the land, so he learned how to take care of wild game meat. As I grew up, he taught me some of his secrets.

Most of the wild meat we ate at the ranch was pronghorn. He always said the best time to take an antelope was in July.

In 1947, I went on my first antelope hunt. I had been on several hunts with my father before he died in 1942, but that was before I was old enough to hunt.

He always said, "Never leave the field before you clean the goat." He said there seemed to be an oil in the hide that came into the meat when it cooled. This oil is what gave the meat the strong odor and bad taste when cooked, he said.

I have always remembered this, and whenever I bag an antelope, I immediately field dress, skin and wash the animal.

In the 45 years I have been hunting, the only bad antelope meat came from one that was shot in the paunch. I have never found a way to get good meat from a gut-shot antelope.

Many people have told us they can tell antelope meat when they taste it. Maybe they can, but most people who eat at our table think our antelope meat tastes like venison.

My sons started hunting with me in 1971. When the season starts, antelope are first on the list. Between the three of us, we have worked out a system of cleaning an antelope that has never failed.

To make things easier, we made a stand about seven feet high out of one-and-one-quarter-inch pipe. We have a horizontal bar about one foot down from the top. This bar has a ring at each end to hang the carcass. We welded a bolt at the bottom to fasten it to the trailer hitch. Commercial skinning racks are available if you don't want to make it yourself.

When the kill is made, we hang the field dressed animal by the hind legs and skin it all the way down to the neck. We cut the head off and wash the inside of the carcass, removing any blood and hair. We then place the carcass in a bag made from an old bed sheet. The sheet keeps the flies, bees and dirt off the meat. At the same time, the meat will cool. We tried commercial game bags, but they didn't keep the meat as clean as we like.

Even if the animal has run for a long distance, this technique should produce great-tasting pronghorn.

In areas where the sex must be attached to the carcass, we leave the head attached. We bring the bag up under the hide to where we stopped skinning, tie it off, and pull the hide over the head, leaving the carcass open to cool. If we don't want to keep the cape, we cut it off and leave just the head attached.

Walter Jenkins
Upton, Wyoming

Trailing Tips

When tracking a wounded animal, I never walk directly over the tracks. My experience has showed me that I may have to backtrack to pick up the trail again.

Joe Mackins
Brookville, Pennsylvania

Hog Hunting Heaven

I hunt in a place where there are quite a few hogs, but sometimes they just don't come to my stand. Here's a trick I discovered that will bring hogs in close.

I take a post hole digger and dig a three- to four-foot deep hole. I fill it about half full of corn, then take one-half gallon of buttermilk and pour it over the corn. Then I fill the hole with dirt and I let it sit there and sour. Then I wait. The hogs go crazy over this.

Before you try this, check to see whether baiting hogs is legal where you hunt.

Jonathan Hubbard
Houston, Texas

A Secure Kill Tag

Have you ever lost your game tag off your animal while dragging it out? I now carry a piece of kite string in my pocket. I tie the kite string through the hole in the kill tag, then roll the kill tag up and push it down inside the animal's ear. Then I pierce the ear, pull the string through it, and tie it to the antler. Now I can drag all I want and the tag won't come out.

Of course, first check game regulations to see whether this tag placement is legal where you hunt.

Larry Hubbard
Belleville, Michigan

Caring For Meat

To keep flies from landing on skinned big game I use a cheesecloth game bag and an electric fan. If it is a hot day, the addition of a gallon jug of frozen water inside the body cavity will help cool the meat.

This simple arrangement works very well. To limit air drying of meat, I do this only for a day or two.

Dod Nobel
Ravenna, Ohio

A Waterproof Tag Holder

In many states, the carcass tag issued with a big game license is not adhesive backed.

In order to attach the tag to the animal for transport, I keep a plastic bag in my hunting pack, along with a roll of electrician's tape. When I need to tag my animal, I simply fill out the tag, insert it in the plastic bag and attach it with electrician's tape to the antler or leg as specified in the regulations. This protects the tag from the weather and allows it to be removed easily for inspection by a game warden.

Keith A. Lengkeek
Douglas, Wyoming

Hunting The Deep Woods

Anyone who hunts the deep woods probably knows that most of these areas have been logged at one time. I have found that most logging roads go downhill and end up at a larger logging road and eventually at a road.

However, in some areas the road may be overgrown. If that is the case, I look for where the new growth is shorter than the surrounding trees. If I can find evidence of logging operations (i.e., stumps) I look around at the skyline. The trees above the old logging road will be shorter than the surrounding woods. I spent a year in Maine when I was in the service and an old-timer showed this to me.

Charles Clark
Ransomville, New York

How To Approach Downed Game

Any big game that has been shot should be approached from behind. I touch the eyeball of the animal with my gun barrel. If the animal is dead, there is no movement of the eye. If the animal is not dead or just unconscious, the eye will blink.

Walter T. Reich
Aurora, Colorado

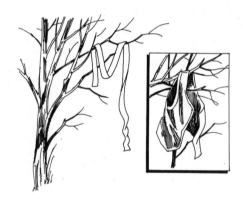

Relocating Downed Game

Sometimes, it is necessary to leave game and get help from your hunting partners. Since blaze orange is very visible, a large blaze orange "marker" left close to the animal can be a great benefit in finding the spot when you return.

We have found this method works very well, particularly as the light starts to fade.

Gordon J. Poppitt
Westminster, California

Use A Bow-hunter's Face Cover

Much can be learned from the bowhunting fraternity. The "mask" or face cover is one very obvious accessory that benefits the rifle/shotgun hunter.

I have found its advantages in providing camouflage for the face, plus it keeps bugs and flies away from my face and neck. A face mask also prevents sunburn and even keeps cool breezes from becoming a nuisance.

Gordon J. Poppitt
Westminster, California

Sunglasses Can Help
Spot A Blood Trail

It is well known that a Coleman lantern helps illuminate a blood trail under low light conditions. I have discovered that it is easier to locate blood spots during the middle of the day, if I wear sunglasses with built-in ultraviolet filters.

Gordon J. Poppitt
Westminster, California

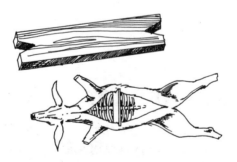

Rib Cage Spreader

I keep a three- by nine-inch piece of wood with a "V" cut in each end in my hunting vehicle. I use it to spread the rib cage of game, which helps speed the cooling process. This device can be used year after year.

Jim Lammerding
Havre, Montana

How To Spot Game

Several years ago, I learned a trick while hunting elk in Washington. The friend I was hunting with had taken about 40 elk.

We were glassing a bowl with dense timber. My partner spotted elk within a few minutes. They were in the timber. I kept looking and looking. Finally I found them. I then asked how he spotted the elk so fast. His tip was not to look for just elk. Instead he focused on the color of their rumps.

Today I find that a majority of my elk sightings start with yellow rumps. Then the elk materialize.

Wyndle Wright
Frisco, Texas

How To Judge A Rack

A tip I learned in British Columbia while elk hunting was how to count points quickly.

We were hunting a six-point area only. My partner showed me a diagram of a elk rack and counted out the tines by name. All elk racks are basically the same up to the fourth tine, which is the sabre or royal tine.

He taught me to start counting tines at this point back instead of at the head. At 1,000 yards, this little trick saves time.

Wyndle Wright
Frisco, Texas

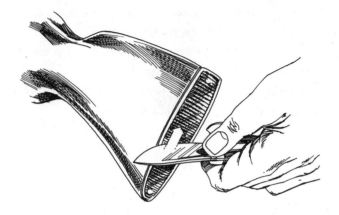

Grandpa's Squirrel Trick

Here is a squirrel hunting trick my grandpa taught me. I use it when I am under a tree and a squirrel is hiding on top of a limb.

I take out my hunting knife and gently rub the blade against the butt of my rifle or shotgun. This makes a light scraping sound. I sit for about two minutes in complete silence. Eventually, the squirrel will poke his head out, offering me a shot. This has produced many squirrels for me.

Kevin Boehm
Zionsville, Indiana

Tree-stand Squirrel Hunting

If I can't seem to get close enough to chattering squirrels, I use a tree stand. I hike in early, climb into my stand and wait them out.

Squirrels pay no attention to me. After I take a shot, I keep quiet and don't move. Soon the rest of the squirrels in the area will get back to their routines.

Steve Kosek
Bellaire, Ohio

Coyote Transport Bags

I hunt coyotes on the plains of Colorado. To keep from getting the carpet in my vehicle dirty, I carry a box of 39-gallon lawn bags. These are large enough to handle even big coyotes and I don't have a mess to clean up when I get home.

I also carry Hertz 2-in-1 flea and tick powder. When I shoot a coyote, I dust it liberally with the powder. I also put some powder in the trash bag. That way I don't have to worry about getting fleas on me while I'm skinning the coyote.

Joel Fleischer
Lamar, Colorado

Squirrels And Sunshine

I plan my squirrel hunt ahead of time. I work the timber so that I will have the sun at my back during the early morning and late afternoon. Squirrels are active during these times, and this strategy affords much better visibility.

Wayne E. Kampmeier
Bolivar, Missouri

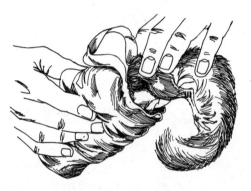

A Clean, Scent-free Pack

When I am hunting small game I use plastic sacks to wrap the game in before putting it into my hunting pack. This keeps my hunting pack clean and scent-free. When I get home, I simply wash out or throw away the bloody plastic bags.

I do this because I use the same hunting pack for small game that I use during the bow-hunting season.

David Loman
Waltonville, Illinois

The Invisible Helper

I have found that squirrels often stay on the opposite side of the tree, where I don't have a shot. To solve this problem, I take a roll of fishing line and tie it to a bush behind the tree. I walk to the other side, then tug on the line. The squirrel then runs to my side of the tree.

Patrick Thomason
Warren, Arkansas

35

Squirrel Stones

I carry a few small stones when squirrel hunting. If a squirrel is hiding on the opposite side of a tree, I pitch a rock on his side. The sound will cause him to jump around the tree to my side.

Amos S. Gingerich
Paoli, Indiana

Better Rag Decoys

When winter winds get too strong, Texas rag decoys tend to slap around and the sound could easily flare incoming birds. The best solution I have found is to stitch up the bottoms. I leave an opening of about three to four inches for the stakes. This also gives the decoys a more bird-like shape.

Benjamin Breeden
Leavenworth, Indiana

Cheap Decoy Weights

I was tired of losing expensive lead decoy weights, and concerned about leaving spent shell casings behind. I found a solution to both concerns.

I take 12- or ten-gauge spent shell casings, mix up a little concrete and fill the casings. I add a twisted loop of light wire to each casing for an efficient, affordable decoy weight. Several will hold a decoy in deep water on the windiest day.

Earl Barton
Council Bluffs, Iowa

Better-tasting Birds

Carrying uncleaned birds in a game bag can harm the flavor. On warm days, I field dress birds immediately by cutting a crosswise slit at the vent and removing the guts with a hook made from a branched twig. This gets out most of the innards.

Amos Yoder
Morley, Michigan

Recovering Arrows

Bow-hunting small game can be fun and can help sharpen shooting skills. However, sometimes I am hesitant to cast an expensive arrow at a squirrel. Here's a technique that has proven to be effective for me.

When shooting at squirrels, I use flu-flu arrows to keep my arrows from going too far. After shooting and missing (which is the normal result for me), I pull out my compass and set a bearing on the direction of the arrow's flight. I follow my compass setting to the arrow. Flu-flu arrows land fairly close and are easy to see.

Sometimes I use blunt-tipped arrows to keep from sticking the arrow into a limb.

Tim Slover
Rogersville, Missouri

Liven It Up

When the ducks have been shot at a few times and the water is calm, the ducks get wary. I use a little trick that makes my decoys move without paying extra money for the motion decoys that run on batteries.

I tie a weighted line from the decoy to the bottom of the water, then I run a line from the decoy to my blind. When I call the ducks and they hesitate to land, I move a few of the decoys. The ducks see this movement, which helps bring them in.

Josh Adams
Gresham, Oregon

The Multiple-blind Approach

My love and passion is hunting waterfowl. I have spent over 15 years enjoying it. I live in southeast Tennessee, and in an area we call "No Birds Land." Because we are located between the Atlantic and the Mississippi flyways, we do not see the number of birds most people do. Therefore, we have changed the way we hunt.

Most people hunt from one blind. If we did that here, the ducks would soon pinpoint our blind and move to another place. Our solution is to line up a number of hunting spots, and change our location often. We never hunt more than two days in a row at the same place.

We scout, then set up a blind. The next day we move to another location. People have talked me into returning to the same blind several days in a row. We ran the ducks off and never had a good shoot in that spot again.

Mike Tipton
Calhoun, Tennessee

The Mobile Approach

Being a mobile duck hunter puts the odds in my favor. Instead of being tied to a blind in one location, I move as the birds move. For instance, if the weather turns cold and the sloughs start to freeze, I move to a better spot.

When it gets cold, ducks leave the frozen places and head for open water. Instead of staying home, the mobile hunter can still hunt. During extremely cold temperatures, I find open water in rivers and on large bodies of water.

Mike Tipton
Calhoun, Tennessee

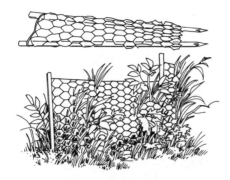

A Cheap Portable Blind

Here in Western Kentucky, a lot of duck hunting is done in sloughs or backwaters. The majority of this water is relatively shallow. Although a permanent blind provides many luxuries, when temperatures drop below freezing the water begins to freeze and a permanent blind is almost useless.

My cure was to build a temporary blind that could be moved as the water freezes. Here's how I built a cheap portable blind.

1. Cut four two-inch diameter wooden poles six to eight feet long; sharpen one end.

2. Purchase common chicken wire and cut two pieces. Staple each piece to two poles, one pole on each end of the chicken wire.

3. Weave brush, weeds and camo cloth into the wire.

4. Roll up each section for easy transport.

When I get to my hunting spot, I push the poles into the ground, forming a shape similar to a football. Then I take brush, limbs, etc., and make a little cover for the top. This blind can be left in place and moved as frequently as needed. Only a new top needs to be made each time.

Although this blind costs very little, it will provide excellent camouflage. At season's end, always pack out all man-made blind material.

J. T. Harris
Murray, Kentucky

41

A Real Fly-down Sound

A turkey wing from a previous hunt can be used to simulate a bird leaving its roost. I simply roll my sleeve up and rapidly slap the wing against my bare forearm. This is a more authentic sound than slapping the wing against my thigh. Check your regulations to make sure this is legal in your area.

John Ford
Bethel, Utah

42

Protect Your Box Call

Just because it's raining doesn't mean I stop turkey hunting. When using my favorite box call in wet weather, I simply take along a plastic bread bag. This keeps the call dry and sounding great. I use it, then slip it back into the bag.

Ron Hollnagel
Boscobel, Wisconsin

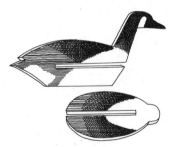

Home-made Goose Decoy

Commercial goose decoys are expensive and bulky. I make my own. To make a good goose decoy, I cut two goose silhouettes out of cardboard or thin plywood—a side view and a top view. I cut a slot in the middle of each, slide them together and paint the decoy.

In the field, the wind will cause the decoys to move side to side, imitating the movement that geese will flock to. I cut the side view into both feeding and attention positions. When taken apart, I can carry or store hundreds of them.

Nate Katzenmeyer
Travis AFB, California

A Faster Decoy Setup

For a faster decoy setup, I anchor decoys in an angle out from the shore line and downwind. I place another small group of decoys upwind from the end of the long line. This leaves a space in which the ducks can land.

When I hunt over this setup, ducks telegraph their intentions quickly as they follow the long line into the open area.

T. Ken Malcolm
Dauphin, Manitoba

44

Leg Slaps Can Imitate A Hen

When calling spring gobblers from the roost, I use a leg slap in conjunction with the "fly-down cackle" very successfully. Here's what I mean:

I set up as close as I can without spooking the bird. I prefer about 100 yards. I set up with my back up to a tree with no undergrowth. I let the woods settle down from my movements. Then, I start calling with soft yelps. I call so soft that someone 15 feet away could just hear me.

I will hear the chirps and songs of birds now, and maybe the gobbler has cut loose. Gradually I increase the volume of my calling. I call just loud enough to let him know my location. At this time I call about every five to ten minutes.

Here is where the leg slap with the cackle comes into play. I start with about six sharp putts followed by a cackle. I may do this several times depending on how the gobbler is responding, but more than three times is probably too much.

Now I take my bare hand and slap on the bottom of my thigh four times in quick succession. This sound imitates turkey wings slapping together as the bird flies off the roost. I pause for two seconds, then shuffle my feet in some leaves. This adds to the illusion of a hen coming off the roost.

On several occasions I have had gobblers fly off their roosts to within 20 yards of me. But not all gobblers react like this. No tactic works every time, but try this next spring and add some realism to your calling.

Steven L. Fitzgerald
Lakeview, New York

Making A Trail

If I find a roosted gobbler I want to set up on the next morning, I mark a trail using a roll of reflective tape. On my way out, I mark a tree every 50 yards.

Early the next morning when I shine my flashlight, it's like having a row of lights leading straight to my spot. When I leave the woods I collect the tape.

Bill Metzing
Poplar Bluff, Missouri

My Best-kept Secret

I hunt ducks in flooded timber and on private land. Sometimes, I walk up to two miles to reach my hunting spot. On these hunts I use Feather Flex decoys. These are foam, half-body decoys that weigh only a few ounces and can be collapsed for easy transport.

I load a couple of dozen decoys into my back pack. I have shot over the same decoys for years and they are still going strong.

Mike Tipton
Calhoun, Tennessee

46

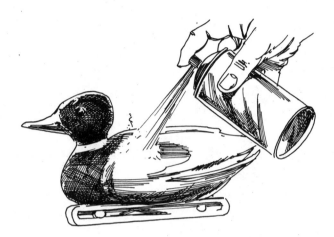

Saving Decoys

Paint wears off duck decoys. I delay this from happening by applying a few coats of a spray-on finish to the decoys. I put the decoys on a piece of newspaper and spray a thin layer on each. I let this layer dry for about an hour and then I spray on another thin layer. This coating keeps the paint on for a long time.

Josh Adams
Gresham, Oregon

Buy Different Decoys

Rather than purchasing one type of decoy, I recommend using several different brands and styles. A variety of decoys adds realism to my setup.

Mike Tipton
Calhoun, Tennessee

A Better Decoy Spread

When I am hunting open water and there is the chance to take puddle and diving ducks, I separate my decoys.

I place my puddle ducks upwind of my blind. Puddle ducks use the wind to land and typically land at the back of the decoys. With decoys upwind of my blind, no matter what direction puddle ducks come from, I can still get a shot.

My puddle duck decoys include mallards and gadwalls together, and a few black duck decoys off by themselves. The black duck decoys serve as confidence builders.

I place my diving decoys downwind from my blind. Diving ducks typically land at the front of a decoy spread.

I use bluebill and goldeneye decoys. Red head, ring neck, bluebill and others will decoy to bluebills. Goldeneye, hooded mergansers and buffleheads will decoy to goldeneyes. I use a large number of magnum decoys, with twice as many bluebill decoys as goldeneyes.

Mike Tipton
Calhoun, Tennessee

49

Weapons

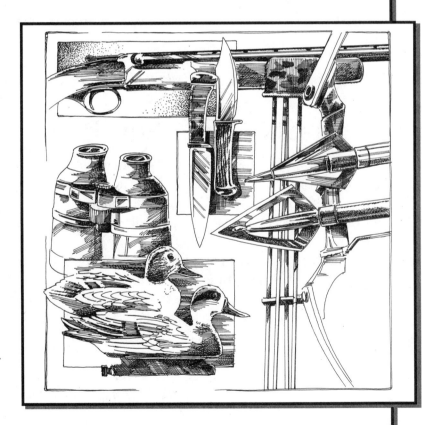

A Cheap Rust Inhibitor

I keep a small cloth sack full of anhydrous calcium chloride in my gun case as a moisture inhibitor. It's cheap and can be bought at most drug stores. This keeps my equipment from rusting.

James A. Moes
Holland, Michigan

Shoot In A New Rifle

A new rifle must be "shot in" before it will achieve its full potential.

When I buy a new rifle, I buy 200 rounds of ammunition and spend a day at the range. I repeatedly fire five rounds, then clean the bore.

After 100 rounds, I move up to ten rounds between each cleaning. This helps the rifle bed into its stock, the barrel and receiver to mate properly and the bolt to loosen up. The constant cleaning will season the bore so that dirt is less likely to stick to it. I sight in my rifle after 200 rounds.

A. H. Mattson
Battle Ground, Washington

An Affordable Bipod

Here's an inexpensive, homemade bipod I use for ground hog hunting. Compared to a commercial bipod that attaches to a rifle's forearm, this one is very inexpensive and weighs only a few ounces.

I have had very good luck using this homemade device. Anyone can make it with very little effort and money. Here's how to build one:

1. Start with two one-half-inch hardwood dowels measuring 36 inches. Nine inches from the end of each, drill a one-eighth-inch hole.

2. Align the hole in each dowel and insert a one-and-one-half-inch-long #10 bolt through the hole. Screw a wing nut on the bolt.

3. Slide one-half-inch diameter plastic tubes (measuring six inches each) over the top part of each dowel.

4. Sharpen the bottom end of the dowels to prevent the bipod from slipping on hard ground.

I use this bipod when the grass is too tall for a prone shot. I place the forearm of my rifle in the "V" section above the bolt. My elbow rests on my knee. This rig is very steady.

When walking, I can stick one leg of the bipod through my belt loop for easy transport.

George Curtis
Fredericksburg, Virginia

Take Extra Targets On Your Hunt

I always keep some paper targets or pattern sheets in my vehicle. I never know when my gun or scope may be knocked out of alignment in a fall or other mishap. It is frustrating to try and find something to help re-sight it in.

I also keep a spare topographic map in my car in case something happens to the one I take afield.

Rick Baggett
St. Louis, Missouri

Get A
Better Grip

Hunting requires quick reflexes. That means a good grip on the gun stock. I use a dozen rubber bands to improve my grip.

I twist rubber bands around the hand piece until they are tight. After the hunt, I take the rubber bands off so they don't damage the stock.

Steve Kilgore
Grand Ledge, Michigan

A Portable Reloading Table

Because of a job that requires moving every two to four years and living in an apartment, I found that space for reloading equipment and a reloading bench had created a problem.

The answer was a metal tool chest with a piece of three-quarter-inch plywood mounted on the top. The tool chest provides a stable work space. The strong metal drawers provide adequate space and storage for dies, bullets, powder, etc. The plywood top provides a place to mount my reloading presses. The lock feature is great for security and safety, and the large casters help with moving and storage.

Gregory L. Copley
Bismarck, North Dakota

Gun Protection

I use a plastic garbage bag to keep my rifle and scope dry. I stick my rifle barrel into one corner and wrap the rest around the rifle. My rifle slips out easy.

My two sons and I have hunted much territory over the years. We always carry a garbage bag in a pocket.

Lester Tuttle
Washington, Kansas

Always Pack A Bore Sight

Large airports require a hard case to transport firearms. However, the handling of these cases by airline baggage handlers is sometimes less than gentle. Due to rough handling between flights, a scope can be knocked off zero. For this reason, I always pack my bore sight.

I simply check my sight in before I leave and make a graph as seen in my bore sight. Upon arrival in camp, I pop the bore sight back in and check for the same graph reading. This can save a missed trophy because the scope was off. This graph is taped inside my gun case for easy reference.

Phillip Jenkins
Mertens, Texas

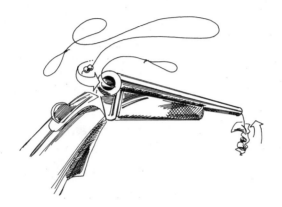

An Inexpensive Cleaning Rod

While I was growing up my father was overseas in the military. I started hunting and didn't know what a cleaning rod was. I used 10-pound fishing line with a piece of cloth that was just big enough to go down the barrel. My guns were a .22 caliber and 20-gauge.

On one end of the line I would tie the cloth; on the other end I would attach a split BB shot fishing weight. The weight would pull the line down the barrel. Then I pulled the cloth through. The first couple of times I would put a couple drops of oil on the cloth. Then I would run a clean cloth down the barrel. The fishing line should be two to three inches longer than the barrel.

Danny D. Shirah
Dothan, Alabama

Better Accuracy

A problem I have in shooting tight groups is gun oil in the barrel. Gun oil is necessary for prolonged periods of storage, but this same oil can cause poor bullet placement.

My solution: Before shooting my rifle, I clean the bore with an electrical contact cleaner. This removes oil from the barrel, and my groups are tighter. I apply oil after shooting for storage. The contact cleaner does not harm my gun.

Phillip Jenkins
Mertens, Texas

A Cheap Barrel Cleaner

After a long day of hunting, it is easier to clean my shotgun by cutting a patch out of an old t-shirt and tying a piece of thin rope around the middle. I apply some powder solvent on the patch and pull it down the barrel. I do this twice up and twice down the barrel. It removes all light dust and powder coatings in the barrel. This is much easier than the rods and patches.

Roger Johnson
Riverside, California

Barrel Protection

When hunting in snowy conditions, I put a small balloon over the end of my gun barrel. This keeps the snow out. Before I shoot, I simply slide the balloon off.

Lee Remisburg
Post Falls, Idaho

Simple Insurance

I carry a multi-sectioned cleaning rod in my hunting coat or day pack. A few years ago, after taking a shot at a nice buck, I noticed the empty case was still in the chamber of my rifle.

A broken extractor left me unable to deliver a follow up shot. Fortunately, a second shot was not needed. Since that experience I have carried a cleaning rod just in case.

Harold Bennett, Jr.
Wayne, West Virginia

Spray-On Snow Camo

I was hunting geese in a snow filled corn field. To cut the glare and to camouflage my shotgun, I sprayed on "white snow" (that stuff that is used for decorating windows during the holidays). This white snow cleaned up easily with a wet cloth.

Mike Conner
Canton, Ohio

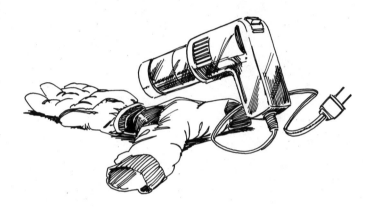

Pack A Blow Dryer

When on a short hunting trip where a power source is available, I pack an inexpensive blow dryer. It can easily dry the receiver and trigger group. A blow dryer can also be used for drying socks and gloves, and thawing frozen locks.

Donald W. Lister
Streamwood, Illinois

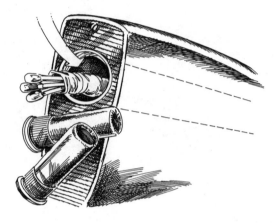

The Invisible Emergency Kit

Most shotguns have a 1-inch diameter hole bored into the buttstock from the butt to about eight inches from the action. This hole is necessary to allow the insertion of a socket and wrench extension to permit disassembly. This hole is normally covered by the buttplate, and serves no other function other than to lighten the buttstock slightly.

I use this hole to store emergency gear. The hole will hold a small compass, a tube of wooden matches and more.

I remove the buttplate and wrap the emergency items in thin padding to prevent annoying rattles. I slide this gear into the hole and reattach the buttplate. I now carry an invisible emergency kit every time I hunt.

Donald R. Bronk
Wausau, Wisconsin

62

Shoot Better and Save Money

For rifle or pistol proficiency, there is no better practice than simple "bull's-eye shooting" at targets. Practicing with an air gun is one of the most affordable ways to become a more skilled marksman, no matter what type of shooting or hunting you enjoy.

Crosman Corporation
East Bloomfield, New York

An Affordable Gun Sling

A simple, affordable gun sling is available at most stores that sell climbing gear. I purchased plastic buckles and one-inch wide nylon webbing to make a sling almost identical to the one that came with my Ruger 10/22.

I decided the proper length for the sling. Then I cut the webbing and used a match to melt the ends so they wouldn't fray. For about $2, I now have an adjustable sling that is strong and will make those long walks back to the truck seem a little shorter. It also keeps my hands free for carrying ducks, dragging deer, or holding hands with my wife on the way out.

Jeff Siscoe
Winner, South Dakota

Easy Stock Repair

To remove a dent from a wooden gun stock, I cover the area with a moistened cloth and press it with a hot iron. The steam will raise the dent. Next, I smooth the steamed spot with fine sandpaper. I follow that by rubbing the dent lightly with steel wool and, if necessary, refinish it to match the color of the stock.

Nathan Ashbaugh
Greensburg, Pennsylvania

A Better Sight

Seeing the bead sight at the end of the barrel in low light conditions can be difficult. My solution is to place a small drop of fluorescent paint on the bead or front rifle sight. I use a small brush or a cotton swab for best results.

Dan Lappin
Lafayette, Indiana

Homemade Target

I make easy-to-read, long-range targets from plasterboard. When hit, the targets give off a puff of white powder that can be seen from a great distance with the naked eye.

Boyd Dial
Bennion, Utah

Pack Your Iron Sight

While hunting elk in Colorado, I fell on a rock and damaged my scope. Back in camp I took off the broken scope and put on my iron sight. I sighted in the rifle, and finished my hunt with the open sight. That iron sight saved my trip from becoming a total loss.

Leonard G. Rockwell
Monterey, California

66

Reduce Sun Glare

Particularly in very early morning and late evening when the sun is low, deep shadow movements are missed because of glare on the eyes or on the binoculars or scope front.

For the eyes, a cap pulled down low helps. It is best if the underside of the cap's bill is black or dark green. Most blaze orange caps have this same bright color on the underside. Use a black felt pen to cover the underside to improve low light vision.

For optics, I use a simple hood for the front lens. I use a piece of plastic tubing measuring one-and-one-half inches in diameter, painted black.

Gordon J. Poppitt
Westminster, California

Less Expensive Shooting Gloves

When shooting powerful handguns at the range or when plinking, I use a pair of inexpensive weight-lifting gloves. Weight-lifting gloves are padded and absorb a lot of recoil. They cost one-third to one-half as much as shooting gloves, and are available at most department and sporting good stores. Shoot more, spend less!

Glen Healey
St. Ann, Missouri

Tips For That Big-game Rifle

Find a big-game rifle that closely matches your .22 long rifle. Look closely at the Remington 700 and Winchester Model 70. Shoot the new rifle every chance you get, so shooting is as easy and natural as possible.

Also, look into reloading while you're at it. Learning how to reload your own cartridges, while expensive up front, can make shooting more affordable once your reloading equipment is in place.

Chad Shirely
Campbellsville, Kentucky

Long Shot Accuracy

When taking a long shot with a rifle, I often reduce shakiness by taking aim slightly below my target and slowly raising the rifle until the sights line up on the bull's eye. I fire as the target is attained.

If you can make this work on paper, try it next time you make a long shot on game.

Robert J. Taufen
Uniontown, Washington

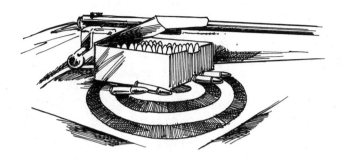

Tips For That First Rifle

If you are just starting to shoot, I recommend that your first rifle be a .22 long rifle, bolt action. Start with a carton of 500 rounds. Find a safe place to shoot. Place targets 50 to 75 yards away, then shoot. Shoot standing, kneeling, sitting and prone.

When 500 rounds are gone, get 1,000 more. Shoot as much as you can, every day if possible. Find a farmer or rancher who wants his rodents thinned. You will get better.

When you can hit the black on the target, start pacing off yards (one long step is about one yard). Pick a spot, guess the yardage, then pace it off. Try 25 or 50, then go to 200. It is important to be able to estimate yardage. Do it often.

Then try some long shots. For these, take a deep breath, let half of it out, and hold the rest as you squeeze the trigger until the round is fired. If you have trouble holding your breath until the gun goes off because the sight will not remain steady, stop. Take a few more breaths, then try it again. You will soon get the hang of it. This technique is used for target shooting and long-range hunting.

Robert J. Taufen
Uniontown, Washington

Avoid Magnum Rifles At First

I know several people whose first big game rifle was a magnum caliber. Today, they are so afraid of the recoil that they flinch and do not shoot accurately.

One man I know said his magnum was inaccurate. Since I knew that his gun was almost new, I tested a theory of mine. I asked this hunter to give me his rifle and one round. I laid the round on the side of the rifle, tipped it into my hand, and closed the action on an empty chamber.

I handed him the rifle and asked him to shoot at a cardboard box placed 30 yards away. When he pulled the trigger, he nearly fell over. When I explained that this happened because he flinched, he asked how to cure it. I told him to buy 10,000 rounds of .22 rifle ammunition, and not to touch his .300 until all the .22s were gone. He said he didn't own a .22. I suggested he get one.

Robert J. Taufen
Uniontown, Washington

Securing Bow Screws

I put a small drop of a non-permanent thread locker on the screws of my bow sight, quiver and rest. Then I tighten them up. They remain tight. If an adjustment is needed, the seal can be broken easily without damage to the screws. I make my adjustments until my bow is back in tune, then repeat the tightening process for a trouble-free bow season.

Jan Housenga
Clinton, Iowa

Breathe Life Into Old Feathers

I shoot only feathers on my arrows. When feathers become matted and worn, I often use my stove and a tea kettle to save the time and expense of refletching.

I just hold the arrow and rotate the feathers over the spout of a steaming tea kettle. The feathers will regain their long-lost youth.

Jesus Ortiz
Los Angeles, California

71

A Better Peep Sight

I have a peep sight that sports a rubber tube stretching from the sight to my bow limb. Once, that little rubber tube broke and slapped me in the face.

Now, before each use, I wipe rubber protectant on the tubing. It penetrates the rubber and keeps it soft and like new. I now get through a whole bow season without a problem. When next season rolls around, I put on a new tube.

Jan Housenga
Clinton, Iowa

A Simple, Cold-weather Arm Guard

Bowhunting in cold weather usually means contending with bulky hunting clothes. This can result in bowstring contact along the inside edge of your bow arm. Bowstring contact with anything during the shot will ruin accuracy.

I have found that arm guards tend to compress clothing material equally around the arm. This leaves a lot of bulk on the inside of my forearm. My solution is to pull all extra sleeve material to the outside of my forearm. I use two or three large safety pins to pin the extra material to the outside of my forearm. The material on the inside of my forearm is kept perfectly flat.

Keith R. Kamrath, DC
Hutchinson, Minnesota

Keep Broadheads Sharp

If I hunt in a region with humidity, rain or snow, I drag the sharpened edge of my broadheads through bowstring wax. This wax protects them from any moisture and keeps them sharp.

Orland Hustad
Scottsdale, Arizona

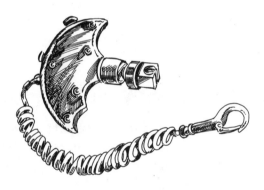

A Dollar Release Keeper

A little gadget called a "coiled chain" has saved my bow release from being left behind. A coiled chain is a plastic cord like a telephone cord. One end of it snaps to my belt loop. The other end attaches to my release. This $1 product has saved my $40 release many, many times.

Al Marohn
Pickett, Wisconsin

Razor-sharp Broadheads

Getting broadheads sharp enough for hunting can be difficult. First, I use a sharpening stone and carefully hone both sides of each edge. Second, I rub the edges of the broadheads on a strip of leather to remove any burrs.

Travis Wooley
Rushville, Indiana

Follow Every Blood Trail

When I go into a thicket and the blood trail gets thin, I get out my squirt bottle and spray it around where I think the game went. In the bottle is a mixture of two parts water and one part hydrogen peroxide. If there is blood on the ground, the peroxide will foam. I then can continue to follow the blood trail.

If it is too dark to safely blood trail game, this technique will still work the next morning.

The peroxide is also handy if you get a small cut or scratch. Just spray some on the cut and it will disinfect it until you can get to camp and clean the wound.

Orland Hustad
Scottsdale, Arizona

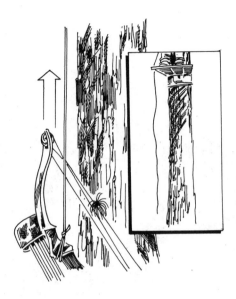

A Dual-purpose Scent Wick

When bow hunting from a tree stand, I use a small diameter 20-foot rope to haul up my bow. I keep the haul rope in a plastic bag with a cover scent such as raccoon urine. After I haul up my bow, I let the rope hang. It works as a scent wick. After the hunt, I roll up the rope, seal it in the plastic bag and add scent as needed.

Glen Healey
St. Ann, Missouri

A Use For Broken Arrows

I use my bent or broken arrows as scent dispensers and to mark distances from my treestand. I cut them to about 18-inch lengths and take them with me on scouting trips. Once I find a location, I stick the shafts into the ground at ten, 20 and 30 yards.

When I use that stand during the archery season, I place a cotton ball in the nock, then place my favorite scent on the cotton ball.

Claude Quick, Jr.
Belvidere, Vermont

Bow String Wax To The Rescue

I frequently switch field tips and broadheads. Often, I experience loose tips. I have alleviated this problem without adding another item to my bag of extras.

Whenever changing tips, I cover the field tip or broadhead threads with bowstring wax. This wax goes on easily and doesn't add a new scent to the bow or myself. I have never had a tip loosen once I applied bowstring wax.

Michael Simons
Linden, Iowa

Practicing Range Estimation

To be ready for bow season, I estimate distances to various objects and then pace off the distance to them. I always try to pick a rock, tree or some other common object.

When estimating the range to a game animal, I am more accurate if I estimate the distance to an object next to the animal (a rock, tree, etc.). If I focus on the animal, it may appear larger or smaller than it really is, and my distance estimation will be off.

Ted A. Graham
Nebo, North Carolina

No-sweat Moleskin

    I have a problem with sweaty palms when it is hot or when I see a deer and get nervous. I am 19 years old and live in Georgia.
    I discovered that placing a layer or two of moleskin on the hand grip gives me a comfortable grip that absorbs sweat.

Marsh Letson
Forsyth, Georgia

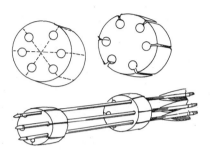

A Cheap Arrow Holder

Every spring, I retrieve my arrows from storage. Usually the vanes are crushed or disfigured from contact with other arrows so I end up refletching them. To save time and trouble, I made a cheap arrow holder.

I bought an ethafoam tube from a toy store (it looks like a pool toy for kids). It is about three inches in diameter, about five feet long and cost about $2. I cut it cross-ways into two-inch pieces. I drew three lines equally spaced through the center of the piece. Next, I drew a line across these lines one-half inch from the edge. I used a very sharp one-quarter-inch drill bit to bore through the cross marks. Next I cut the side of the piece centered on the hole and parallel to it, cutting through the hole about one-quarter to one-half inch. The hole size will vary with arrow diameter.

Then I took two of these discs and snapped the arrows into place. I rotated my arrows until none of the vanes touched. The entire assembly will stand on its own. I use different colors to denote what size shaft I have stored.

Richard Smith
Lexington, South Carolina

Keep Broadheads Sharp

I found long ago that if I want my broadheads to remain sharp, I must place a fine coat of petroleum jelly on the sharpened edges. This will keep blades sharp during long periods of storage.

I fully believe this makes for greater penetration as well. I also place a fine coat of petroleum jelly on the first four inches of the arrow shaft.

Robert E. Mason
Spencer, Indiana

An Easier Draw

I find that placing a two- to three-inch piece of colored electrician's tape on my bow string keeps my arrows from sliding. It provides a good, easy-to-see nocking point and it reduces finger fatigue.

Ryan Foltz
Shingle Springs, California

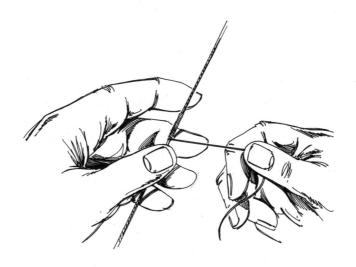

Added Bowstring Life

To give the serving on my bowstring extra life, I wind dental floss where my release causes wear. When the floss wears down, I simply put more on. Also, by putting floss on my string above the nocking point, my nock doesn't creep.

Don Looman
Zeeland, Michigan

Recovering Bucks After Dark

In many cases, the last half-hour of legal shooting is the most productive. When I get a late afternoon hit during bow season, I follow these rules:

1. Monitor the deer's escape route by sight and sound from my stand.

2. Wait ten to 15 minutes before moving from my stand. Unless I am 100 percent sure the game is dead, I do not follow. Even fatally wounded game will run if pushed, often leaving a poor blood trail.

3. As quietly as possible, I leave the area by a route that is opposite where the deer was last seen or heard.

4. After safely storing my bow in camp or in my vehicle (to avoid violation of game laws) I allow for one to two hours to assure death or major stiffening.

5. I return to track game with a fluorescent hand lantern. I have found this type of light makes the blood trail glow in the dark, especially in the outer fringes of the lighted area.

Thomas Galbraith
Cape Coral, Florida

Building The Right Muscles

Here's how I keep my muscles in top shape. Four weeks before seriously practicing, I start drawing my bow eight to ten times with each hand. I do about three sets with each hand. This rebuilds shooting muscles in my arms. I continue this exercise throughout the bowhunting season.

When hunting, I draw my bow at least once every hour in two or three different positions to keep my muscles limber.

Randy Reed
Charles Town, West Virginia

Fletch Spiral Is Important

When buying hunting arrows, I discovered the correct vane spiral is important. As viewed from the rear of the arrow, a left-to-right spiral is for right-hand shooters. A right-to-left spiral is for left-hand shooters. Choosing the correct spiral will produce more arrow spin, better control and greater accuracy.

Phillip Miller
Oak Forest, Illinois

When You Can't Hunt

There are probably very few bowhunters who haven't tried to force a hunt even though the conditions (especially wind direction) were not right. One solution is to set up stands for at least two wind directions. Hunt from the stand only when the wind is right.

However, some days simply dawn with terrible conditions for bowhunting. On those days, here's what I do:

1. Scout new areas.
2. Practice shooting.
3. Repair arrows.
4. Plan a trip. Do map work, correspondence, packing list, etc.
5. Acquire permission to hunt a new area.
6. Sleep (it may help you stay awake on the stand later).
7. Do something for your spouse (it pays).

Tim Slover
Rogersville, Missouri

A Cheap Feather Protector

My solution to shooting feathers in the rain is simple and inexpensive. I bought a shower cap made of thin plastic with elastic on the bottom. They are available in a variety of colors. I take the cap and snap it over my feathers. This keeps my feathers dry in all weather conditions.

Ronald Weidlick
Easton, Pennsylvania

A Cheap Powder and
Bullet Holder

I go to photo labs and pick up clear, round film canisters. I use hot glue and glue two of them together, bottom to bottom. I put powder in one and bullets in the other. I carry this powder and bullet holder in my possibles bag.

G. Brown
Oklahoma City, Oklahoma

Avoiding Misfires

Have you ever had a black-powder gun fail to shoot or delay for two or three seconds before the powder burns? I have.

I now leave my gun outside in the cold overnight and then load it when I get to my hunting spot. The result: It is always ready for a great shot. I have never had it fail since I started doing this.

Jeff Davis
Freeland, Michigan

Game Bags Must Breathe

I have found that carrying small game or upland birds in a game bag makes it much easier to continue hunting. Some possibles bags are equipped with a small game pouch.

Whether I carry game in my possibles bag or in my coat's game pouch, the key is that the game bag must breathe. This is important so that air can circulate and help cool the game animal.

Christopher W. Cooper
Indianapolis, Indiana

A Balloon For Black Powder

    I hunt with a black-powder rifle. On more than one occasion my load has been ruined by moisture. I have lost two good chances at large deer because the loads became damp.

    I now slip a balloon over the end of the barrel. It is cheap and ensures that my loads stay dry. Before firing I take the balloon off.

Billy G. Hannah
Strawberry Plains, Tennessee

87

A Great Possibles Bag

Whether the day's activity is sporting clays at the firing range, small game hunting or hunting deer, I've found that a large canvas purse with shoulder straps is a great possibles bag.

It is large enough to hold all the auxiliary equipment used with front-end loaders or a limit of birds, rabbits or squirrels. There's even room for a sandwich and a small thermos. Most canvas purses have two compartments and many have side pockets.

Christopher W. Cooper
Indianapolis, Indiana

An Affordable Cleaning Solution

An effective and inexpensive cleaning solution I use on muzzle-loaders is made from equal parts of rubbing alcohol, hydrogen peroxide and Murphy's Oil soap. This solution has not harmed my wooden stocks and it has not caused any rusting of my muzzle-loader's metal parts.

Ted A. Graham
Nebo, North Carolina

Load 'Em Up

Here's a little tip I've found helpful when going to the range to shoot my muzzle-loader. I save 35mm film canisters. The empty plastic canisters work great for storing measured powder or Pyrodex.

I measure out a dozen or so, then bring them along when I go to shoot. The little canisters keep my powder dry and work great for pouring the powder down the barrel.

Jerry Bade
Hawks, Michigan

89

How To Remove A Stuck Cap

I always carry a small pair of surgeon's forceps in my possibles bag for removing spent percussion caps that are stuck on the nipple. Surgeon's forceps work better than a knife and are less likely to scratch the gun's finish.

Ted A. Graham
Nebo, North Carolina

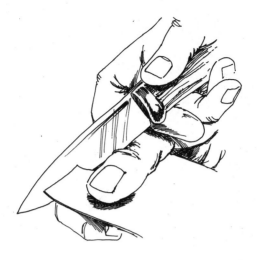

A Safer Way to Notch Your Tag

The majority of states have changed to weather-proof big game tags. Hunters must remove the appropriate notches for date of harvest.

Some tags recommend notching this information with a sharp knife. With the successful hunter already excited by taking the animal and the sharpness of the blade, it is not uncommon for the hunter to cut a finger. To avoid this possibility, I carry small folding scissors or a small nail clippers to remove the notches.

These items fit readily into the hunting pack or fanny pack, and can be carried for a multitude of other reasons, too. The added expense of $1 or $2 far outweighs the cost of bandages (or possibly stitches). The scissors are easy to handle, even with rubber gloves.

Gordon J. Poppitt
Westminster, California

Equipment

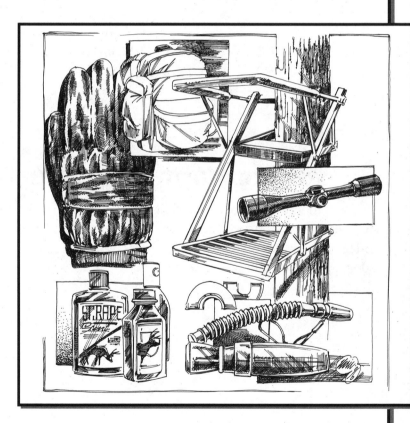

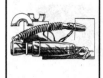

Comfortable Boots

If my boots are tight around the ankles, they will slide on much easier if I put a piece of waxed paper around the heel when the boot is half on. A piece around the heel can also prevent blisters.

Corey Hashem
Berwick, Maine

Staying Warm Is No Sweat

When walking to my stand, I carry my coat until I get into my stand. Then I put on my jacket and gloves. This keeps me dry inside and warmer on stand. It also limits perspiration and body odor.

Jerry Przybylski
Fountain City, Wisconsin

Recycle Old Hip Boots

Don't discard your old hip boots.

I cut off the bottoms at the ankle and use the tops for brush buckers. They are waterproof and briar proof. I use them with my favorite footwear.

M. Homer Feidler
Jamestown, New York

Quiet A Noisy Zipper

To quiet a noisy zipper, I moisten a bar of odorless soap and rub it into my pack's zippers. I work the zippers back and forth to get the soap into the teeth of the zipper. Doing this will reduce the sound the zipper makes. I always open the zipper slowly.

Also, I wrap duct tape on the pull handles to prevent rattles. It's easy and inexpensive.

Jack J. Teer
Hicksville, New York

96

A Clothes Bucket

To help keep hunting clothes scent free, I put them in a five gallon bucket that has an airtight lid. I dust each article with baking soda, turn them inside out and shake the bucket. When I take them out to wear, I shake off the extra baking soda. When putting clothes back in the bucket, I add more baking soda.

Steve D. Otto
Dauphin, Pennsylvania

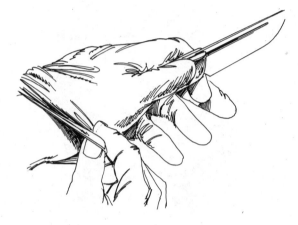

Field Dressing Gloves

Hunters often field-dress game without the benefit of warm water to clean their hands. I usually ended up cleaning them off with snow or in a stream.

To eliminate this problem, I visited my local pharmacy and purchased a box of latex exam gloves. By putting them on prior to cleaning a game animal, I keep my hands dry and clean. After I am done, I remove them and place them in a plastic sandwich bag to dispose of later.

You might get a few odd looks the first time you use them around your hunting buddies, but they will be asking to borrow a pair after they see the results. Not only do they keep my hands clean, they also provide added protection from infection.

Keith A. Lengkeek
Douglas, Wyoming

Footwear Comfort

I roll my socks down over my boot tops once or twice. I wrap the laces around the socks and tie securely. This keeps my socks up and my feet comfortable.

Terry Holifield
Ellisville, Mississippi

A Sturdy Clothes Box

Most of us know that to keep our clothing scent free, we must store it in some type of plastic bag. The problem I always have is that the bag splits open.

Instead of using a large plastic bag, I use a large plastic storage box from the local hardware store. I like the larger, flip-top one for plenty of gear storage. Not only can I store my clothing (scent free), but also my other hunting accessories (fanny packs, knives, extra socks, gloves, safety belt, etc.).

Kurt Schirado
Bismarck, North Dakota

A Bargain Camouflage Outfit

For an affordable camo outfit, find a pair of the military's battle dress uniform (BDU). Try pawn shops or military clothing stores.

These clothes offer plenty of pockets (especially the cargo pockets in the pants), an adjustable waist (great for wearing over thermal underwear) and tear-resistant fabric. There's a cold-weather version and a warm-weather version. I suggest cold weather BDUs because they hold up better against briars. They typically cost $10 to $20 a pair.

Also, invest in one good pair of suspenders to counter the effect of lunch, ammo and other gear stuffed into the cargo pockets.

Adam Stroup
Blue Mountain, Alabama

The Peroxide Solution

Here is how I get blood out of my hunting clothing without discoloring the fabric. I presoak the spot with peroxide. It will foam up like it does on a cut.

After it foams, I put it in the washing machine and wash like normal. It works great. As with all spot removers, always pretest a small spot.

Craig Baker
Midland, Michigan

Warmer Feet

On very cold mornings in my tripod stand, my feet get cold within an hour. Sound familiar?

A friend of mine who is a guide told me to buy some unscented antiperspirant spray and spray my feet before I put on my polypro liners and wool socks. It works. My feet didn't sweat walking in, so they were drier and I stayed warmer.

Wyndle Wright
Frisco, Texas

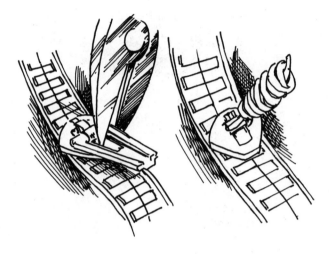

Quieter Zippers

I find it annoying when the zipper pulls "tink-tink-tink" while I am trying to be quiet.

To solve this, I cut the zipper pulls off with a pair of side cutters and replaced them with small nylon wire ties. I tightened the wire ties to the size of a nickel and cut off the excess. Nylon wire ties may be purchased at most auto parts stores or hardware stores.

Randy L. Wadlow
Lake Havasu City, Arizona

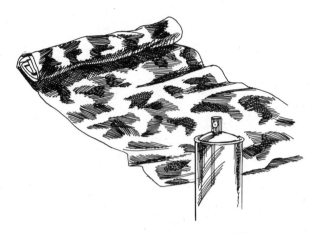

Cheap Camouflage

Instead of buying expensive camouflage netting or screens, I went to my local hardware store and ordered a roll of burlap. I used the factory brown as a base camouflage. Then I spray painted the burlap to make a unique camo pattern.

Arthur W. Duggas, III
Easton, Connecticut

A Solution To Cold Hands

A problem I have is keeping my hands warm. Big gloves may keep my hands warm, but they are too thick to shoot a gun or a bow.

Of all the gloves I have tried, none have worked better than a pair of latex medical gloves. I put them on first, then put on a pair of regular jersey gloves. My hands have never been warmer, and I can still shoot a gun or bow.

Jason Beck
Danville, Indiana

103

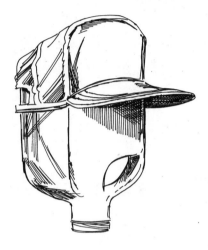

How To Clean A Favorite Hat

I wear a hat quite often. Years ago, I neglected to wash my hat because when it came out of the washer it was a mangled mess. And after it dried, it didn't look or wear the same.

Here's a solution to that problem. I invert a one-gallon plastic milk jug and position my hat (after washing, of course) over the bottom of the jug so that it looks the way it would on my head. I make sure everything looks right to ensure a nice looking hat when dry. That's it!

Now my favorite hat looks and feels good even after washing.

David A. Block
Rockford, Illinois

A Tip To Stay Warm

This may sound crazy, but it works.

My dad told me this tip a long time ago. One Saturday morning, it was 18 degrees outside. I dressed in a cold-weather outfit, plus a pair of coveralls and a jacket. Then I tried to pull my bow back, but couldn't. I could barely walk wearing all those clothes.

Then I remembered the tip my dad told me about. I went to my sister's dresser and got a pair of her old panty hose. I put them on with a pair of blue jeans, and dressed in a lighter outfit. I fired up the old truck and left.

That day I killed my first deer with my bow. The panty hose kept me warm.

Odes Deela
Wilburton, Oklahoma

Simple Whitetail Bait

Where baiting is legal, a simple and inexpensive way to bait a deer stand is to plant a few rows of sugar beets. I till up a narrow strip near my stand where I know the deer enter the field and plant two to three pounds of beet seeds.

As the beets grow, the deer will eat the tops, leaving the beets underground undisturbed. The tops will grow back within a few days and will continue to do so all summer long until a hard frost. Once the frost has killed the tops, I dig up a few of the beets each time I go to my stand and leave them there for the deer to eat.

John Ford
Bethel, Vermont

An Effective Wash

With the washer set on the regular wash cycle, I wash clothes using a scent-free and dye-free liquid laundry detergent. I do not use a powdered detergent. During the rinse cycle, I add one cup of white vinegar and let it soak for ten to 15 minutes; then I finish the rinse cycle. White vinegar will remove any odors and any soap left in the clothes.

I hang these clothes to dry and keep them away from any odors. When the clothes are dry, I put them in a dark garbage bag and add a cover scent or attractant. The clothes will absorb the scent. To make this easier, I make up scent bottles and put them into the bags.

Donald Carlisle
Brownville, New York

How To Ensure
Scent-free Equipment

Most hunters agree that controlling human odors may be the single most important precaution to take when hunting big game. My hunting partner and I have developed a way to keep all of our hunting clothing and small gear scent free.

On a black bear trip in Ontario, we had 72-quart steel-belted coolers in which we planned to store the meat on the trip home. Like most hunting camps, this one was full of smoke during nonhunting hours, so we put our clothes, fanny packs and small hunting equipment into the airtight coolers. I then cut some spruce branches and placed them in the cooler. The clothes took on the scent of pine. What a perfect cover scent!

We now use the coolers during the entire deer season. They work great for transporting the clothes to and from the hunting area. Also, when I load the truck for a hunt, I simply grab my cooler. All my hunting gear is inside, so nothing gets lost from week to week.

We deer hunt in hardwood forests, so we put anything from acorns, leaves, oak twigs, fox urine or deer urine into the cooler. At the end of the season, we simply wash out the coolers.

Scott Olthoff
Dyer, Indiana

107

A Scent Frisbee

    I like to put out deer attractants. Instead of using the popular "scent bomb" (cotton balls stuffed into an empty 35mm film canister), I use a small piece of foam soaked with my favorite scent. With a five-inch long string, I tie this foam to the top of a small camouflaged frisbee.

    I can fling the "scent disk" to the appropriate yardage without contaminating the area with my scent. A frisbee is also easier to find. I use a flexible rubber frisbee that can be rolled up and put into a plastic bag for future use.

Turk Jones
Georgetown, Texas

108

Natural-smelling Clothes

Hiding human odor is an important element if I want to bring home tasty venison. Like most hunters, I wash my camouflage clothes in scentless detergent and use masking scents.

Here's an extra step I use to create more natural-smelling clothes. After I wash my clothes, I dry them with pine cones and pine needles. The pine smell penetrates the clothes and works better for me than a simple cover scent.

Franklin H. Smith, III
Raleigh, North Carolina

Apple Cover Scent

I don't deer hunt much anymore because my husband passed away, but here is one of my favorite tips.

Just before the deer season, we saved rotten apples. We kept them in a mesh bag (the kind potatoes come in). Before walking to our stands, we stepped on the apples and the scent would be on our boots.

Gladys Strothcamp
Sullivan, Missouri

109

A Cheap Deer Feeder

Deer feeders on the market today cost from $60 to several hundred dollars. I found a cheap alternative at the local hardware store for less than $7.

I bought a ten-foot long, four-inch diameter PVC pipe ($5), a cap for the end ($1), and a piece of rope (less than $1). I leaned the pipe against a tree and tied it tight. I left the top end low enough so I can unscrew the cap and load the feeder with corn, beans or any other type of feed. As the deer eat the feed, more feed flows out of the pipe.

One ten-foot section will hold approximately 50 pounds of corn. Another option is to cut the ten-foot section in half for two 25-pound feeders. I spray painted a camo pattern on the feeder.

Of course, first check regulations to determine whether baiting is legal where you hunt.

James J. Hurst
St. Charles, Missouri

Cover Scent Basics

A cover scent must be appropriate for the area I'm hunting. And it must match my hunting style.

I use apple scent only if I'm hunting near apple trees. Apple scent will be unnatural in the middle of a pine plantation. Also, if I'm hunting from a tree stand, I use a cover scent of an animal that would climb a tree, like a raccoon. If I'm hunting from a ground blind, then I use a fox scent.

Rick Baggett
St. Louis, Missouri

An Easy Scent Dispenser

To kill my scent when hunting white-tailed deer, I take a piece of cotton and pour on a little of my favorite scent. I place the cotton on the sole of my boot with a thumb tack. I do the same on the other boot. This seems to kill my scent and attract deer.

Tim Trabish
Somerset, Kentucky

III

An Old Deer Attractant

Here is one of the oldest tricks in the book to attract deer. Where legal, I put out some peanut butter close to my stand. Deer love peanut butter. As long as I put out peanut butter, the deer come.

Check game regulations first to make sure baiting deer is legal where you hunt.

David Fuquea
Chickamauga, Georgia

A Cheap Cover Scent

For a simple cover scent, I find a cedar tree and trim the soft green tips off the branches. I put them in a blender with water and puree until it is a liquid. I strain this mixture through panty hose into a plastic spray bottle.

I spray this on my clothes before hunting, and carry it with me to spray on limbs or foliage.

Dennis Hoddy
Ponca City, Oklahoma

A Natural Cover Scent

When I am out scouting or hunting, I grab a cheek full of young wild onions. They have a surprisingly pleasant, mild taste and they double as a great cover scent.

Steve Kosek
Bellaire, Ohio

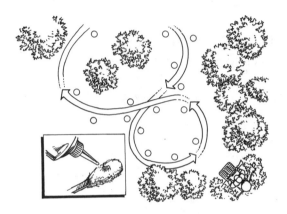

Dispersing Deer Urine

After finding a suitable tree for my stand, I spray deer urine on a cloth or boot and walk a figure eight approximately 50 to 75 yards away from my stand.

Then I use six-inch, cotton-tipped applicators with a wooden shaft and soak them with deer urine. I place the applicators in the ground 20 yards from my stand where I have a clear shot. I use three to four applicators in front, behind and to each side of me. Deer often stop and smell the cotton applicators.

When it rains the urine dissipates, so I soak a half dozen applicators and throw them (or shoot them with a rubber band) around my stand. I have harvested many deer using this method.

Ed Bonner
Canonsbury, Pennsylvania

A Free Cover Scent

If you hate to spend money for a little bottle of scent, here's a cheap alternative. My dad owns a confinement building. Whenever I go hunting, I step in the building and get the hog smell on me.

This is easy and cheap. Deer smell hog all the time in our area. This is an effective, affordable cover scent.

Matt Beach
Leonard, Missouri

A Local Cover Scent

If hunting in a pine forest, I put my hunting clothes in a garbage bag overnight with a cotton ball soaked in turpentine.

If I am hunting in oaks or maples, I rake up some leaves and put some in a garbage bag with my hunting clothes. If I smell like the natural surroundings, I will be less likely to spook deer.

Jack Dunbar
Lake Tomahawk, Wisconsin

A Simple Skunk-scent Carrier

I believe skunk tincture is a great cover scent. Unfortunately, it has such a strong scent that it can be smelled even when the bottle is closed. In order to transport it in the truck without leaving a bad smell, I bought an airtight plastic container to carry the bottle.

To keep the bottle from rattling around, I went to a craft store and bought a Styrofoam ball slightly larger than the diameter of the container. I cut the ball in half, then cut a hole in the center just large enough for the scent bottle. I pushed one piece of the Styrofoam into the container. Now the bottle fits inside with no rattles, spills or smells.

With the second piece of Styrofoam, I cut a hole in the center and camouflaged it with cloth. In the field, I set the bottle in the hole and don't have to worry about the bottle tipping over on uneven ground.

Joel Fleischer
Lamar, Colorado

Scent-free Steps

I use steps to climb trees. To get rid of the oily smell, I take some chestnuts and crush them. I put them in a pot and boil them for 15 minutes. Then I soak my tree climbers in the water for a day. This rids the climbers of that oily smell.

Jason Whitmore
Vermontville, Michigan

A Cheap Scent Delivery System

Apple scent never seems to stay around long enough. My solution during a long hunt is to fill a couple of plastic sandwich bags with apple juice. I put a rock in each bag and then seal them.

When I want to renew the apple scent I just throw one of the bags away from my stand. The bag breaks open and leaves fresh apple scent. At the end of the day I retrieve the plastic bags.

Scott Chevalier
Menominee, Michigan

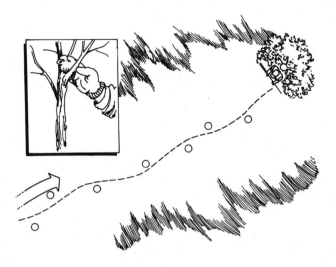

Build A Scent Wall

Building a scent wall is an ideal technique to ambush a buck in rut. I have taken deer with a gun and bow from ground blinds and tree stands using this technique.

I look for an open ridge that gives me good visibility, yet is narrow enough that I can shoot across. I prefer a ridge where the wind blows horizontally across the opening.

I start at the top of the ridge and place a scented cotton ball three to four feet above the ground in a small bush or tree. The cotton ball is scented with an attractant. I walk down the ridge, placing cotton balls five to ten feet apart.

I apply a cover scent to myself, then get into position upwind of the scent wall. Depending on available cover, I sit at the top or the bottom of the ridge. Bucks in rut are attracted to the scent wall.

David Howard
Farmington, Arizona

Put Deer At Ease

I wear a blaze orange vest when hunting deer. Some people don't wear blaze orange because they fear deer will see the orange color and leave.

My solution is to put an orange stool or orange vest in my tree stand before and during the season. This allows the deer to get accustomed to the orange. I find this really works.

John Martin
Commerce, Georgia

Tree-stand Comfort

Sometimes when I'm in my tree stand I drop my hat, camouflage veil or glove. Rather than leave it on the ground where deer may pick up the scent, I retrieve it without leaving my stand.

I simply take a piece of string and tie a large fishing lure on one end. I like top-water lures best. I lower the lure to the dropped item, snag it and pull it back up to my stand. This saves me the task of climbing down the tree.

James B. Wells, Ph.D.
Lexington, Kentucky

A Quiet, Camouflaged Chain

To quiet my tree-stand chain I dip it in liquid rubber. Liquid rubber is available at most hardware stores. This quiets and camouflages the chain.

I found that black or brown works best. I put several thin coats on the chain by dipping it, hanging it to dry and then dipping it again. If you try this, make sure the chain links do not glue together when drying. Also, do this two to three months before you plan to use the stand to allow the smell to fade.

Andy Butzler
Deer Park, Wisconsin

"Whooo" Can Quiet The Squirrels

When deer hunting from a tree stand, I have been bothered by pesky squirrels. Once they locate my position, they bark and carry on until every deer in the woods knows where I am.

I have a solution. Once I spot a squirrel, I hoot softly like an owl. They disappear without a sound. The owl must be a natural predator of the squirrel. Also, the sound of an owl hoot does not seem to alarm deer.

Jan Housenga
Clinton, Iowa

A Hunting Dummy

About one month before the archery deer season opens, I place a dummy in my tree stand. The deer get accustomed to seeing "someone" in the stand. When I am in it they pay no attention to me. After hunting in the stand, I put the dummy back in it. In the past three years, several deer have been harvested from this stand during the archery, blackpowder and rifle seasons.

Jay Laxton
Sayre, Oklahoma

Carry Rocks For An Easy Escape

Sometimes I get caught in my tree stand at dark with deer everywhere. The question is how do I get out of my stand without spooking the deer and revealing my hunting location?

My trick is to carry a few small rocks in my pocket. If I am caught in my stand after legal shooting hours, I throw the rocks away from my stand. The noise will spook the deer. When they hop away, I get out of my stand and leave.

Ben Tilberg
Wisconsin Rapids, Wisconsin

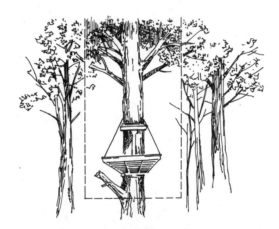

Build A Blind With Cut Limbs

During archery season I create shooting lanes by cutting tree limbs. I take the clipped limbs and place them behind and to the side of my tree stand. I tie or wedge the limbs into place. With proper camouflage, I will completely blend in with my background.

Bill Metzing
Poplar Bluff, Missouri

121

Equipment

A Quieter Approach

I use an ordinary yard rake to clear leaves and debris from the deer trail to my stand. I start raking a narrow path about 30 to 40 yards before my stand so that I don't give away my stand position. This helps me make a quiet approach.

Shane McNamara
Pictou, Nova Scotia

A Cheap Seat

I took an old pair of camouflage pants and cut off the legs. I sewed the bottom openings closed, and filled the seat area with pillow stuffing. Then I sewed the waist opening closed. This made a cheap, comfortable camouflage pillow for my tree stand. I use the pockets by putting hand warmers inside. This makes a great, inexpensive hot seat.

Joey Lamiano
Highland Lakes, New Jersey

Two Lights Are Better Than One

I can save a lot of time and hard work by carrying two flashlights to my tree stand. If I shoot a buck just before dark, I turn on one light and set it in my stand.

I start tracking the animal with my second light. If I made a good shot, I should find the deer within sight of my tree-stand light. By the time I tag and field dress the deer, it will be dark. I head straight back to my stand with the deer. From there, I can drag the deer on the trail. This is easier than using my compass and dragging the deer over rough terrain.

Bruce DuLong, Jr.
Mohawk, Michigan

Quiet A Noisy Chain

I have a tree stand that uses a chain to grip the tree. That chain rattled and banged whenever I carried it afield and set it up. To reduce that noise, I took a small rope and thread it through each link. I then tied off each end. This helps quiet my tree-stand chain.

Chad Baker
Hoxie, Arizona

123

Camouflage A
Tree Stand's Bottom

For total camouflage, I look at my tree stand from the ground. I paint or mask any part that is brightly colored or reflects light. Also, I look at the bottom of my boots. That bright yellow Vibram tag on some boots can be easily covered.

Rick Baggett
St. Louis, Missouri

Multiuse Hand Wipes

I take baby wipes in a plastic bag into hunting and fishing camps. They can be used to clean hands after gutting animals or fish, as toilet paper or as a wash cloth for a bath.

Mike Christenson
Valdez, Arkansas

124

Cheap Screw Locks

If your screws work loose on your hunting equipment, add a drop of fingernail polish. I just put some on the threads and turn it in. It holds it tight and will keep the screw from backing out. However, I can still remove the screw if I want to.

John Yoder
Patriot, Ohio

A Better ATV Box

I use plastic storage containers on my ATV racks to hold hunting and camping equipment. It became a hassle to constantly remove the tie-down straps every time I wanted something out of the box. To remedy the situation, I attached four short rubber cords to the sides. This allowed the box to be securely fastened to the ATV rack, while leaving the lid free to be opened and closed.

Here's how I did it: Start with four short rubber cords and remove the S-hook from one end of all four. Next drill two holes on both ends of the container about two inches from the top edge. Then run a carriage bolt through a washer, through the hole in the cord and through the hole in the container. Inside, attach another washer and finally a nut.

I have found that crisscrossing the cords holds the box most securely. For transporting the case while not on the ATV, I hook the cords across the lid. This keeps them from dangling and catching on brush.

David Russell
Groveport, Ohio

Scope Magic

Have you ever seen a whitetail in the brush, but couldn't find him in your scope? Here's my solution: I sight in my target by looking over the top scope adjustment cap. Once I have the target over the cap, I keep my eyes on the target and bring the crosshairs up to my eye.

This took a little practice, but once I got the hang of it, it really helped.

Dennis Dignall
Cochranton, Pennsylvania

Reuse Chewing Tobacco Tins

Most people just throw away empty chewing tobacco tins. I reuse them.

I paint them with camouflage colors and store my small turkey hunting items in them. I have one that holds my box call chalk and slate sand paper. Another holds my diaphragm calls.

I have one in which I keep .22 cartridges for when I'm out plinking. They are small and quiet. By reusing them, I keep plastic out of the landfill.

Rick Baggett
St. Louis, Missouri

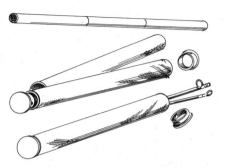

A Cheap Rod Tube

Many hunters bring a fishing rod on hunting trips. Here is how I protect my rod without paying a lot for a commercial rod tube.

I bought a PVC pipe and two end caps from my local hardware store. Two-inch diameter pipe works great for most rods. Total cost was about $12. I glued one end cap on, and fastened the other with duct tape.

Rick Baggett
St. Louis, Missouri

The Lightest Anchor

When portaging a canoe to remote locations, I pack a long piece of rope and an empty mesh bag (the kind that fruit comes in). When I reach my destination, I put rocks in the bag and tie it closed with one end of the rope. I have a reliable anchor.

Robert Herda
White Bear Lake, Minnesota

A Cleaner Cooler

I used to loathe melting ice cubes flooding the bottom of the cooler, seeping into food and bags of fresh game. Now I keep an assortment of different size plastic jugs full of frozen water in the freezer. The large chunks of ice last longer than a bag of cubes, and there's never a wet mess in the cooler. If I'm gone for a weekend, I almost never buy ice. Also, as the ice melts, I have a source of ice-cold drinking water.

I use 16-ounce and 2-liter soda bottles. One-gallon milk containers make a big block of ice. Half-gallon milk containers have a tendency to spring leaks.

J. Lynn Currie
Springfield, Illinois

Multipurpose Gun Oil

When I prepared my gear for the opening of coyote season, I thought I had everything. However, when I got into the field, I found out I had overlooked something.

As I climbed out of my truck to go to my first stand, I realized that I had not oiled the door hinge on my truck and it was squeaking. If I didn't fix it, the squeak would announce my presence to every coyote within earshot. Fortunately, I had my field gun cleaning kit, which contained a bottle of gun oil. A few squirts of oil in the appropriate place and I was able to get to the rest of my stands quietly.

Joel Fleischer
Lamar, Colorado

A Moveable Lantern

When setting up camp, I string a line between two trees. Then I put a cord through my lantern's handle and loop it over the line. This allows me to move the lantern easily to the location where light is needed.

Sonny Lewis
Mesa, Arizona

Garbage Bags Have Many Uses

I carry a couple large garbage bags in my pack. In an emergency, I can cut holes for my head and arms for use as a rain jacket. I also can use one for a wind breaker. A white garbage bag can be used to mark downed game.

Mike Christenson
Valdez, Arkansas

129

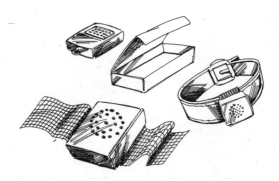

A Low-cost Collar Finder

About three years ago, I purchased a fairly expensive dog training collar. I was deathly afraid of losing the collar in the field if it came off the dog.

I solved this problem with a low-cost solution. I went to my local hardware store and bought one of those key-finders for people who are always misplacing or losing their keys. I got the top-of-the-line model.

I put some silicone sealer around any seams where water might get in if the dog went for a swim. I then made a small holder for the device out of a thin piece of leather. I placed several holes on the face of the holder to keep from muffling the sound when I activated the device. I then made the closer flap and attached a piece of Velcro to keep the flap closed. I used some nylon webbing attached to the back of the holder to enable me to slip the whole thing onto the dog's collar.

When I go to the field, I just slip the activator button in my pocket.

Rick Nelson
Winner, South Dakota

An Easy Truck Cover

I use a fitted sheet to keep the glass on my pickup cab clear of snow and frost in the winter. A sheet also keeps the cab cooler in the summer. The wiper blades hold it snug in front. In back, two small clamps on a thin rope across the pick-up box holds the sheet in windy weather. A queen size sheet is the right size for my truck.

Arvid J. Hushagen
Standwood, Washington

A Cheap, Lightweight Canteen

I carry a 16-ounce plastic soft drink bottle filled with water. It fits in my coat pocket and I barely notice it is there.

Kenneth Trace
Mechanicsburg, Pennsylvania

Cheap Camo

I use a lighter to burn one end of a wine bottle cork. I blow it out and wait a minute for the cork to cool. Then I rub the black ash on my face, neck and hands. The black ash gives a subdued camouflage that stays on, yet washes off with soap and water.

Aaron R. Stickler
Rockford, Illinois

Multipurpose Tape

I carry a roll of black electrician's tape with me while hunting. It comes in handy for a lot of quick fixes while in the field. Here are two uses:

1. When stalking game, I wrap tape around my lower pant legs. It helps quiet my movement through heavy brush.

2. When field-dressing game, I put on disposable shoulder-length gloves and pull them up snugly. I wrap tape at midbicep, and I don't have to worry about the gloves sliding down.

Electrician's tape is a quick fix for short-term problems. Just make sure to carry the tape out of the woods with you when you are through.

Gregory A. Smith
Elizabethtown, Kentucky

Fog-free Binoculars

One problem I have encountered with my binoculars is the lenses continually fog up when I use them. This problem is intensified when I'm wearing a face mask.

To solve this problem, I cut out pieces of clear plastic to conform to the shape of the protective eye area of the binoculars. I cut them to fit snugly over the lenses. This not only helps maintain clear visibility, but it keeps the lenses from fogging up.

Chris Cochran
Oxford, Mississippi

Wax Protects Gear

To protect my gun or bow during wet weather, I coat it with a thin layer of wax. Floor wax works great and sheds water freely. Some brands are scent free.

Shane McNamara
Pictou, Nova Scotia

Stuff That Sleeping Bag

Instead of rolling up a sleeping bag, I stuff it in. I start with an end of the sleeping bag and push it in little by little until the whole bag is inside. I am surprised at how much room is left over, which I use to pack other items such as a pillow or rain suit.

Thomas S. Brink
Plymouth, Wisconsin

A Cheap Binocular Cover

Binoculars are an indispensable tool to big game hunters. The problem is when I am out in all kinds of weather, I must keep water and debris out of the lens.

I have found that a cover cut from a small inner tube can protect both ocular and objective lenses. I tie it to the binocular housing. This keeps the lenses clean and it can be slipped off quickly.

Dennis E. Leveille
North Granby, Connecticut

Day-pack Comfort

Most deer hunters who stay in the woods all day carry a day pack. As I climb around and over obstacles, the shoulder straps keep slipping off my shoulders. This is very annoying. I solved the problem by getting a small elastic cord and placing it from strap to strap across my chest.

Dennis E. Leveille
North Granby, Connecticut

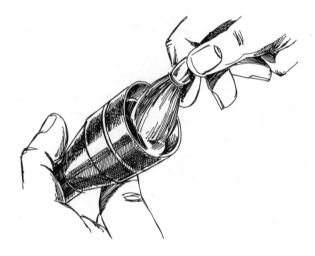

Keep Lenses Dust Free

Keeping scope and binocular lenses clean and dust free, especially while hunting the windy and dusty plains of Wyoming, has been a problem.

Last fall I found a solution. Before leaving for my Wyoming hunt, I asked my wife what she does with those soft brushes she receives with her make-up kits. She told me that she seldom used them and found a couple for me. I found that they are great for dusting off my lenses. I now keep one in a small plastic bag in my pocket while hunting.

Marv Schultz
Green Bay, Wisconsin

A Reticle As A Range Finder

I use the four-plex reticle in my rifle scope as a range finder. I set up an 18-inch square target at 100 yards, then I adjust the scope's power ring until the four-plex brackets the 18-inch target. I note the power setting.

When I find myself looking at a deer at an unknown distance, I turn the scope to that power setting. If the deer's chest fills the four-plex, then it is 100 yards away. If it fills one-half of the four-plex, then it is 200 yards away, and so on. This works pretty well out to about 400 yards.

Rick Morrill
Meeker, Colorado

Tactics

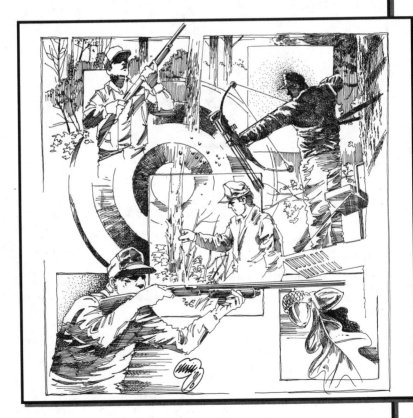

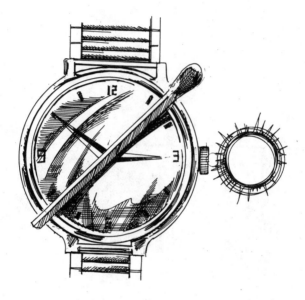

Wristwatch Compass

If I lose my path, I use the sun and my wristwatch to guide myself out.

First, I point the hour hand directly at the sun.

Second, I locate the point between the hour hand and the number 12 on my watch. That point is south.

Third, I use a stick or match to line up due south, and then determine which direction I need to travel.

Jeremy O'Donnell
Wichita, Kansas

Multiuse Dental Floss

Dental floss is a good addition to a survival kit or hunting pack. The uses are endless, from tying off the intestines to protect game meat when cleaning, to tying a splint to stabilize a broken bone. One small container will last for years and it is extremely strong.

I buy waxed dental floss, which seems more resistant to water over time.

Tony Griffin
Bernalillo, New Mexico

Great Balls Of Fire

I carry inexpensive fire starters that I call "Great Balls Of Fire." I use petroleum jelly, cotton balls and a film canister. I rub petroleum jelly into the cotton, and put them into the film canister. When I need a fire, I take out these cotton balls and light them. They burn long, hot and well enough to start a fire in the most adverse conditions.

I make my fire with small material next to the cotton balls. I prefer dry moss, twigs or thin bark. I stay away from green, wet matter.

David A. Elfstrom
Belgrade, Montana

Build A Survival Nest

Imagine this: You are stranded in the woods and it's getting dark. It's drizzling and the temperature is falling. It may take several days for anyone to reach you. You are not cold yet, but you are hungry and wet and you can't find any dry wood to build a fire.

All living things need water, food and shelter. The most critical thing for you is shelter. You can go for days without water and weeks without food. But in your circumstances, you could die from hypothermia in a few hours. Hypothermia is especially dangerous when the temperature is in the 40s and you are wet. At these moderate temperatures, you lose body heat before you realize it. And when you do, it may be too late.

The solution: Leaves and pine needles are good insulation. If I am ever in this situation, I will rake up a pile of leaves, needles and grass next to a bank, a log, a tree or an overhang (preferably out of the wind). Once I have my "squirrel nest" built, I will crawl in and pull the leaves over me. I will still be wet and miserable, but I will stay warm.

Ted A. Graham
Nebo, North Carolina

A Faster Fire

For a faster fire I cut charcoal briquettes in half (the kind that light with a match). I put six to eight pieces in a plastic bag to stay dry. Smaller pieces aren't as bulky to carry. I carry one or two bags when I am hunting. This makes it easier to cook or keep warm.

Lucien A. Escalle
Fresno, California

Downhill Is Often Easier

The best course of action when you are lost is to stay put. Find a sheltered position and make your location visible to rescuers.

But what if no one will miss you? What if no one will come looking for you? Which way do you go?

If I am in this situation, I always go downhill. Sooner or later I will come to a stream. I follow the stream downhill. I will eventually come to a road or railroad. Eventually a road or railroad should lead me toward people.

Cutting across country is probably the worst thing I could do. An added benefit in going downhill is that the walking is easier and I won't travel in a circle.

Ted A. Graham
Nebo, North Carolina

Emergency Tackle

I take a small butane lighter and wrap electrician's tape around the bottom and middle. The tape can be used for all sorts of repairs in the field, or an emergency bandage when used with a piece of cloth. I keep this in my pant pocket.

As an alternative, I wrap tape around the end of my flashlight. In cold weather, the tape keeps the metal from sticking to my lips when I hold it in my mouth.

Jim Lammerding
Havre, Montana

Two Handy Items

Two handy items I always carry with me in the field are a candle and a whistle. A candle burns longer than a match and is much easier to start a fire with. A whistle blast carries much farther than my voice, and lasts longer.

J. E. Cragle
Hunlock Creek, Pennsylvania

A Free Fire Starter

A cheap, effective fire starter is available to anyone with a clothes dryer. I save the lint from the dryer screen and compact it into a film canister. The lint will ignite quickly.

Jim Bailor
Connellsville, Pennsylvania

Last Resort Fire Starter

I have found the clear pitch found in fallen pine trees will help start a fire when all other kindling is too wet to burn. I dig the pitch from the tree's center up under the roots.

James A. Moes
Holland, Michigan

A Cheap Fire Starter

A small plastic pill bottle with a screw cap, filled with cotton balls which have been soaked with rubbing alcohol, serves two purposes.

First, the cotton balls can treat a small cut or wound.

Second, even in a strong wind or snowstorm, the cotton balls light easily and make an excellent fire starter.

Al Marohn
Pickett, Wisconsin

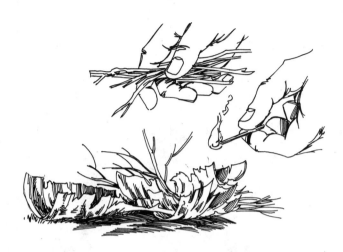

A Natural Fire Starter

Whenever I am stuck in the rain and want to build a fire, I use the outer bark of white birch. The bark has a flammable oil that makes it sure-fire kindling, even when the wood is wet. I do not peel bark from living trees. Doing this scars the tree and may even kill it. If I can't find a dead birch, I use a dry cedar or thin shavings of pine or other resinous softwood.

Nathan Ashbaugh
Greensburg, Pennsylvania

A Pocket Fire Starter Kit

In case I need to start a fire in the field, I carry a used shotgun shell made into a candle, plus waterproof matches and a small roll of toilet paper. This all fits in a small plastic bag.

Kenneth Trace
Mechanicsburg, Pennsylvania

147

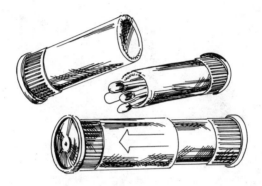

An Inexpensive, Waterproof
Match Keeper

Here is the way I keep matches dry while outdoors.

I take an empty 12 gauge two-and-three-quarter-inch shell and cut the fold off the end. I do the same to an empty 16-gauge shell of the same length. I slide the 16-gauge into the 12-gauge shell and float-test it in a sink or bucket of water. If it floats and no water enters, I have a waterproof match container.

I then put wooden matches in the 16-gauge shell and slide the two shells together.

This is an inexpensive, waterproof container I carry in my pocket, backpack or survival kit. Note that, for some reason, not all shell combinations seal.

Charles Haynes
Ransomville, New York

Recycle Spent Shells

I make candles from empty shotgun shells. They burn a long time and will not break when carried in my pocket or pack. These candles provide a one-match fire when conditions are damp.

Bob Stolberg
Washburn, North Dakota

An Easy Emergency Light

If I happen to be in the woods and must stay overnight, here is a simple emergency light I make.

I need a pop can, a small candle and matches. I take a knife and cut off one-third of the can's side. I make a small hole in the bottom of the can, just large enough to hold a small candle. I make several holes in the top of the can which will allow the smoke to escape. Then I light the candle.

I am amazed at the amount of light the inside of the can reflects. I set the can on a log, stump or tree branch, or hang it by a wire.

Charles M. Clark
Ransomville, New York

A Fanny-pack Survival Kit

A fanny pack makes a perfect survival kit. It is lightweight, small and so comfortable I forget it is there. It will easily hold matches, fire starter, bandages, dental floss, glow stick, knife, space blanket, duct tape, jerky, snake bite kit, fishing line and hooks. I design my survival kit for the area and time of year that I hunt.

Tony Griffin
Bernalillo, New Mexico

Picture Preparation

It only takes a minute to pose a trophy animal for a pleasing photo.

Before gutting and skinning, I fold the front and hind legs under the kill and set it up on its chest and stomach. I make sure its tongue is in its mouth. I shoot the photo from the side with the least amount of blood.

I kneel behind the animal on the opposite side the picture will be taken from, and stay back far enough so that the horns are close to the end of my reach. This makes the trophy look as big as possible. I take a quick look over my shoulder to make sure my background is clear of trucks, buildings, etc. And I always point my rifle in a safe direction.

Now I am ready to take the picture!

Tony Griffin
Bernalillo, New Mexico

An Electric Fire Starter

I need three items to build an electric fire starter: a nine-volt battery, a small pad of steel wool and a ball of lint or other tinder. I place the tinder where I want the fire, hold the steel wool over the tinder, then touch the battery posts to the steel wool. This will ignite the steel wool, which will ignite the tinder.

I always keep a strip of electrician's tape over the posts of the battery, and I carry the battery separate from the steel wool and lint.

Pat Callahan
Modesto, California

Capture The Memories

The time I spend with my children is special. I carry a camera to capture pictures of their youth. I also carry with me a small cassette recorder. It can capture the sounds and excitement of that first hunt and a great trip. These are sometimes sold as "mini" cassette recorders and cost about $40.

Vince Carr
Denison, Texas

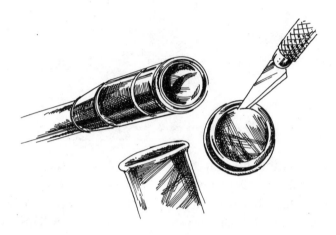

Replacement Eye Protectors

Sooner or later, most scopes lose their rubber eye piece and replacements are often expensive and not readily available. I have found that a cap from an Agfa film container makes a snap-on eye protector for most scopes.

To modify this cap, I place it snugly onto the canister and then carefully cut around the inside rim with a sharp, pointed blade. I trim the inside, and snap it over my scope's eye piece.

Gordon J. Poppitt
Westminster, California

Carry A Backup Compass

The benefits of using a compass, especially in new terrain, cannot be overemphasized. I always carry a backup compass as insurance. I hang one around my neck on a string and tuck it into an upper pocket for easy access.

The other I place in my fanny pack or backpack.

Gordon J. Poppitt
Westminster, California

A Bear-proof Camp

Here's how we keep bears out of camp. On the perimeter of the camp we stretch a rope about two feet above the ground. We soak strips of cloth approximately two feet long with kerosene. Then we hang the strips of cloth on the rope four feet apart. Bears do not like the smell of kerosene.

James A. Moes
Holland, Michigan

Hear It All

This might seem like a strange practice, but it works for me. The night before I go hunting, I sleep with ear plugs in my ears. I don't remove them until I get to my deer stand. When I do remove them, I think my hearing is as good as it will ever be. When I hear leaves crunching in the distance, I can close my eyes and pinpoint where the sound is coming from.

Paul E. Ginter
Collinsville, Illinois

Protecting Guns, Cameras And Optics

I reuse the silica gel packets found in everyday products. These can be used to remove moisture from gun cases, travel vaults and gear bags. They will pick up moisture not found in routine cleaning or maintenance of my gun, camera or optics. Silica gel packets are used in everything from stereo equipment to vitamin jars.

Joseph M. Julian
Chittenango, New York

Better Success Photos

For the best photos of the game animal and me, I tuck the animal's tongue back into its mouth before it begins to stiffen up. Then I wipe off any blood showing or I simply cover it up with my rifle or with foliage.

These two simple steps make my pictures much more appealing. It shows respect for the animal and for any non-hunters who might view the photos.

Thomas S. Brink
Plymouth, Wisconsin

Keep Game Meat Cool

Wild game should be cooled quickly to protect its flavor. Often that means field dressing to get the hot blood and entrails out of the body cavity.

In cases of large animals, I prop the chest cavity open with a stick. During early bow season, I put a bag of ice inside the deer.

When dove hunting, I carry a small cooler with ice. Doves cool quickly and are much better fare than those that ride in my game pouch.

Tim Slover
Rogersville, Missouri

Dog Maintenance

To rid my long-haired hunting dog of burrs, I work a little bit of cooking oil into the tangle. Or, I simply crush the burr. This will loosen the burr so I can comb it out.

Shad Denton
Konorado, Kansas

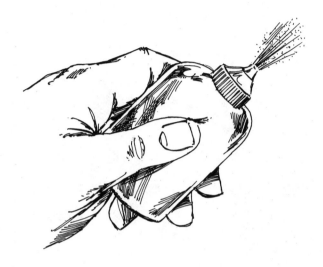

Baking Soda Tips

I carry a small powder bottle filled with baking soda. To determine wind direction, I hold it upside down and squeeze. To wipe a sweaty brow, I wet a handkerchief with water and add a little powder. If bugs start biting, I make a paste and dab a little on the bites for comfort. I do this while in my tree stand or where there is no accessible water by using a little powder and saliva.

Geoff Sidelinger
Scenery Hill, Pennsylvania

157

Keep Meat From Spoiling

Have you ever had waterfowl or other game meat spoil before you got home? Here's what I do: One week before I leave, I fill a large cooler with about four inches of water. I place the cooler in a chest freezer. The water freezes and this frozen chunk of ice prevents spoilage for up to seven days. I keep the cooler covered with a sleeping bag, and I drain off any water.

Robert Hagel
Brainerd, Minnesota

Quiet Keys

When big-game hunting, I pack a roll of duct tape in my vehicle. Just before I leave for the woods, I wrap my truck keys in duct tape and keep them in my pocket for a quiet walk.

Thomas DeWolf
Campbell, New York

An Easy Way To Tell Time

When I hunt out of a tree stand I want to keep my movements to a minimum. However, I do want to keep track of the time. My solution is to push a thumb tack through a hole in the band of my wristwatch and into the tree. I can monitor the time with no movement.

Steve Fuller
Harborcreek, Pennsylvania

A Polaroid Setup

I use a Polaroid camera to set up hunting photographs. I can view pictures minutes after they are taken. This way, I can change settings or angles to get the photo I want. I find this very useful, because I don't get a second chance to shoot pictures once the animal is butchered and in the freezer.

Steve Kosek
Bellaire, Ohio

Dealing With Declination

As a forester, I spend a lot of time cruising timber with map and compass. Magnetic declination was always a chore, especially trying to remember in which quadrants to add and subtract for declination.

For example, in an area with a five-degree east declination, true north 25 degrees east becomes magnetic north 30 degrees east. Meanwhile, true south 25 degrees east becomes magnetic south 20 degrees east. I add the declination in the northeast and southwest quadrants, but subtract the declination in the southeast and northwest quadrants. Of course, if I am in an area with a west declination I do just the opposite.

The simple way to avoid this confusing math is to remember to turn right for east declination and turn left for a west declination. If my declination is 12 degrees east I simply set my compass on the bearing I want to follow and turn the compass 12 degrees to the right. The compass will now be pointing to the true bearing as opposed to the magnetic bearing.

How important is declination? An error of one degree will cause me to miss my destination by 92 feet at a distance of one mile. If my declination is 15 degrees and camp is four miles away, ignoring declination will cause me to miss camp by 5,530 feet; that's more than a mile.

Ted A. Graham
Nebo, North Carolina

See And Hear More

I use a technique I call "splatter vision." It involves blurring my vision. I use it quite often while hunting and almost slip into it naturally (especially when daydreaming). This technique allows me to see more and to detect the smallest movements in my total field of vision.

Also, I hear more without using electronic devices. I learned it from my dog. When she wants to hear something better, she raises her ears and turns them in the direction of the sound. I take my cupped hand and place it behind my ear. I experiment by turning my head. Try this technique, and you will be surprised at what you are missing.

Leo P. Gonnering
Herlong, California

Know The Landscape

When hunting in unfamiliar territory, I turn around and look where I've come from. The frequency depends on the terrain. If I am in the woods, I look back every ten yards. In open areas, I look back every 50 to 100 yards. This helps me find my way back at the end of the day.

Leo P. Gonnering
Herlong, California

Carry A Prepaid
Long Distance Card

I take a pre-paid long distance calling card with me on
hunts. It is nice not to worry about carrying change or other billing
methods if I want to call home or call my workplace. Calling cards
cost as little as $5, and take up very little room.

Rick Baggett
St. Louis, Missouri

Maintain Good
Landowner Relations

When I request written permission to hunt or fish on private land, I find the number one concern of most landowners is liability. I make up my own permission slips and on the reverse side, I include a statement about liability. I find this helps with hesitant landowners.

Stephen L. Gingras
Lowell, Massachusetts

Chemical-free Drinking Water

For safe drinking water without the use of chemicals, I take debris-free water from a free-flowing source, and add one finger size piece of charred hardwood for each quart of water. I use an uncovered pot with lots of surface area, and bring the water to a rolling boil. I boil for at least ten minutes.

I allow the water to cool, then filter out the charcoal pieces. If this water is for drinking, I add one pinch of table salt per quart of water. I stir well, then pour back and forth several times between two clean containers. This restores the air and the taste that boiling removes.

Phillip Miller
Oak Forest, Illinois

A Squirrel-proof Food Cache

To keep squirrels out of a food cache, I place moth balls around the area or by the entrance. This keeps them away from the food.

Jeremy Ellis
Trapper Creek, Arkansas

Cool Refreshment

When I want a cold can of pop after hunting, but don't want to pack it all day, I find a creek that I pass by at the end of the day. I place the can under water and secure it with a rock so it doesn't float away. This provides me with a nice cold drink after the hunt.

Steve Patton
Bloomington, Indiana

Conserve Your Energy

When I have a long walk ahead of me, I conserve energy. Each time I step up on a log or rock, my leg muscles lift the entire weight of my body. This can get very tiring. Unless I'm in snake country, I try to step completely over these obstacles. This saves energy and allows me to hunt that extra hour.

Jonny Novalis
Florham Park, New Jersey

Bug Repellent

If I plan to hunt where mosquitoes, deer flies and horse flies are bad, I take garlic oil capsules. I start taking them three to four days before the trip. Although bugs still swarm around me, I have found that they will not bite. I don't know if this works on black flies or other biting insects.

Ray Roadifer
Litchfield, California

Read, Read, Read

I read all the hunting books I can get my hands on. The North American Hunting Club has great books on hunting. Also, books by Jack O'Connor are good. Jack was a .270 nut. He showed me his collection of mounted heads from animals that he bagged all over the world. He was a wonderful hunting mentor.

My advice is to read books, talk to hunters and ask questions.

Robert J. Taufen
Uniontown, Washington

Tips For Hunter Safety Classes

Before you can get a hunting license, you must take and pass a hunter safety course. When you go, be prepared to learn. Listen to the instructor, and remember what you hear.

Handling firearms is a serious business, and show-offs are neither looked up to nor accepted. Always watch your background when you are shooting. Know where your bullet will go if you miss your target. Good hunters do not have stray bullets flying around.

Hunting is a grown-up tradition. Play it straight. You will find acceptance and great people who will share shooting tips and help you to reach your potential. And you will have a lot of fun in the process.

Robert J. Taufen
Uniontown, Washington

Faster Cleanup

When cooking on an open fire, I rub liquid dish soap on the outside and bottom of all pots and pans. The dish soap will burn, but it will wash off. This protects pots and pans and keeps the metal from turning black.

M. Radtke
Fort Stewart, Georgia

Avoid The Postseason Blues

If I have the blues after deer season I grab my favorite shotgun, a handful of shells and head to the land where I deer hunt.

I hunt rabbits, but during the day I keep an eye out to see what deer made it through the season. I may stumble across some shed antlers. And I may just bag a rabbit.

Joseph (Fletch) Cassini
Muskego, Wisconsin

Index

rag, 37
setup, 44, 49
styles, 48
Deep woods, 27
Deer drag, 2
Deer feeder, 110
Deer urine, 113
Dental floss, 141
Does, 9
Dog collars, 130
Dogs, 130, 156
Downed game, 28
Draw, 80
Drinking water, 165, 166

E

Ear plugs, 154
Electrician's tape, 133
Elk, 20, 31
Emergency kit, 62
Eye protectors, 152

F

Fanny pack, 150
Feeders, 9
Fence-line whitetails, 9, 10
Field dressing, 22-23, 26, 30, 37, 98, 156, 158
Field judging, 31
Firearms, 52, 53, 54, 56, 57, 58, 60, 62, 63, 64, 65, 66, 67, 68,

M

Maps, 20, 161
Matches, 148
Mirrors, 6
Misfires, 86
Moleskin, 78
Mule deer, 2, 20

N

Noise, 6, 15, 16, 17, 119, 121, 122, 123, 159, 162

P

Patterning, 20
Peep sights, 72
Peroxide, 74, 100
Petroleum jelly, 142
Photography, 150, 151, 155, 160
Planning, 84, 168
Portable blinds, 41
Portable reloading table, 55
Possibles bag, 88
Powder, 85
Predator call, 2
Preserving decoys, 47
Pronghorns, 22-23

S

Wind, 11, 14, 19, 20
Wind indicator, 14, 19, 157
Wisconsin deer rope, 2
Wristwatch, 140, 159

Z

Zippers, 96, 102

182

Index